European Social Charter
Short guide

Council of Europe Publishing

French edition:

Charte sociale européenne – Vade-mecum

ISBN 92-871-4309-9

Cover Design: Design Workshop of the Council of Europe
Edited and published by: Council of Europe Publishing
Layout: DTP Unit of the Council of Europe

Council of Europe Publishing
F-67075 Strasbourg Cedex

ISBN 92-871-4310-2
© Council of Europe, September 2000
Printed in Germany by Koelblin-Fortuna-Druck

The Council of Europe

The Council of Europe was founded in 1949, in the wake of the second world war, in order to enhance European construction, based on a common set of values, contempt for which had brought about a time of strife and barbarism.

The Organisation currently comprises 41 member states – in other words almost all the countries of the European continent, representing some 800 million Europeans. Since 1989, the Council has been one of the driving forces in bringing western, central and eastern Europe together. It works towards creating a common democratic and legal area structured around the European Convention on Human Rights. It develops many forms of co-operation on a wide range of issues to be addressed by our societies today, including education, social cohesion, protection of national minorities, the fight against all forms of intolerance, the prevention of crime and corruption, the consolidation of local democracy and the enhancement of Europe's cultural heritage.

Council of Europe Publishing is the official publisher of the Council of Europe, and reflects the many different aspects of the Council's work, addressing the challenges facing European society today. Our catalogue of over 1 200 titles in French and English includes topics ranging from international legal instruments and human rights to ethical and moral issues, society, environment, health, education and culture.

For more information please see our website: http://book.coe.fr

Contents

Part C: Summary of the case law of the European Committee of Social Rights

Foreword

This *Short guide to the European Social Charter* was written by the Social Charter Secretariat of the Directorate General II – Human Rights of the Council of Europe in response to the needs expressed by states having ratified the Social Charter or preparing for ratification.

In particular, the *Short guide* is the result of an initiative taken by the Bulgarian authorities, who at a seminar held in February 1999 within the framework of the ADACS programme voiced their hopes that a book of this type should be published.

Its aim is to provide, in the form of easy-to-consult fact sheets, both concise and accurate information on how the Social Charter's supervisory system actually works and on the main orientations of the case law of the European Committee of Social Rights. A further and just as essential chapter covers the Social Charter's impact on states, during their preparations for ratification or after they have ratified the treaty.

Finally, the three main parts of the guide are supplemented by practical information, including fifty questions on the Charter.

The *Short guide* is also more generally a contribution to the publications of the Council of Europe relating to the European Social Charter, which are intended to give the fullest explanations possible of the functioning and realities of this treaty. The range of publications includes, in particular, the following titles:

- *The Social Charter of the 21st Century* (colloquy organised at the Human Rights Building on 14-16 May 1997);
- *Fundamental Social Rights – Case law of the European Social Charter,* by Lenia Samuel (2nd edition in 2000);
- *European Social Charter – Collected texts* (2nd edition 2000).

In addition, the collection of Social Charter Monographs focuses on different aspects of the Charter, giving summaries of case law and explaining the Charter's influence in various areas:

No. 1: *The family*

No. 2: *Equality between women and men* (2nd edition)

No. 3: *Children and adolescents*

No. 4: *Migrant workers and their families*

No. 5: *The right to organise and to bargain collectively*

No. 6: *Conditions of employment* (2nd edition)

No. 7: *Social protection*

No. 8: *Employment, vocational guidance and training*

No. 9: *Proceedings of the multilateral seminar on the drafting of first reports on the application of the European Social Charter (Strasbourg, 6-8 September 1999)*

No. 10: *Collective Complaint No. 1/1998 - International Commission of Jurists (ICJ) versus Portugal - Documents.*

Finally, more information is available on the Social Charter's web site at: http://www.socialcharter.coe.int.

Secretariat of the European Social Charter
May 2000

Definitions and terminology

Parliamentary Assembly

The deliberative organ of the Council of Europe, composed of representatives and substitutes chosen from each country's members of Parliament.

Community Charter

Declaration adopted in 1989 by the Heads of State and Government of eleven member states of the European Union.

European Social Charter

Treaty adopted in 1961 under which the member states of the Council of Europe, Contracting Parties to the Charter, undertake to observe social and economic human rights.

European Commission

The executive organ of the European Union. It is based in Brussels and ensures that treaty provisions and decisions taken by European Union organs are properly implemented. It has the right to introduce legislative measures.

European Communities

Coal and Steel Community (1951), Economic Community and Atomic Energy Community (1957).

Committee of Ministers

An organ composed of the Ministers of Foreign Affairs of the member states of the Council of Europe.

Council of Europe

An international organisation founded in 1949 and based in Strasbourg, which comprises forty-one European states.

Council of the European Union (or Council of Ministers)

An organ composed of ministerial representatives from the member states of the European Union.

European Council

Regular meetings of the Heads of State and Government of the member states of the European Union.

European Convention on Human Rights

A treaty adopted in 1950 under which Council of Europe member states undertake to observe civil and political human rights and freedoms.

European Court of Human Rights

A court of forty-one judges, based in Strasbourg, which supervises Council of Europe member states' compliance with their obligations under the European Convention on Human Rights.

Court of Justice of the European Communities

A court based in Luxembourg which enforces European Community law and interprets and applies the treaties of the European Union.

International Court of Justice

The United Nations court, sitting In The Hague, which settles disputes submitted to it by states parties and which rules in cases provided for in the Charter of the United Nations.

Universal Declaration of Human Rights

A resolution adopted by the General Assembly of the United Nations in 1948, which recognises the principle civil, political, economic and social human rights.

Organisation for Security and Co-operation in Europe (OSCE)

International security organisation with fifty-five member states. Its objectives are conflict prevention, crisis management, and post-conflict rehabilitation.

European Parliament

The Parliament of the European Union. Its members are elected by European Union citizens by universal suffrage from the member states of the Union.

European Union

Founded in 1992 in Maastricht pursuant to the Treaty on the European Union. Presently comprises fifteen European states.

Part A
Presentation and description of the European Social Charter

The European Social Charter

1. The Social Charter and its Protocols

A **European treaty** opened for signature in Turin in 1961 and entered into force in 1965, the European Social Charter, which protects fundamental social and economic rights, supplements the European Convention on Human Rights which guarantees the protection of civil and political rights.

The Charter is now implemented in twenty-one European states:[1] Austria, Belgium, Cyprus, Czech Republic, Denmark, Finland, Germany, Greece, Hungary, Iceland, Ireland, Luxembourg, Malta, the Netherlands, Norway, Poland, Portugal, Slovakia, Spain, Turkey and the United Kingdom.

Other states have signed but not yet ratified the Charter.[2] These are Croatia, Latvia, Liechtenstein, Switzerland and "the former Yugoslav Republic of Macedonia".

The Charter has been supplemented by three Protocols:

- **The Additional Protocol of 5 May 1988** (Protocol No. 1, Fact Sheet A – 3) guarantees four groups of new rights; it came into force in 1992;

- **The Amending Protocol of 21 October 1991** (Protocol No. 2, Fact Sheet A – 5) or the Turin Protocol, has revised the supervisory system;

- **The Additional Protocol of 9 November 1995** (Protocol No. 3, Fact Sheet A – 7) has provided for a system of collective complaints: it came into force on 1 July 1998.

The **revised Social Charter** opened for signature in 1996, came into force on 1 July 1999 and will replace the 1961 Charter (see Fact Sheet A – 4).

---

1. See Fact Sheet A – 4 for a list of the Parties to the revised Charter.
2. This list includes states which have signed the Charter but not the revised Charter. For signatory states to the revised Charter, see Fact Sheet A – 4.

2. Rights guaranteed by the Charter

The Charter and its 1988 Additional Protocol guarantee a set of fundamental rights related to housing, health, education, employment, social protection and non-discrimination. They may be can divided into two categories:

a. *Conditions of employment*

- Non-discrimination in employment, prohibition of forced labour;
- trade union rights, the right to bargain collectively, the right of workers to information and consultation as well as the right to participate in the determination and improvement of working conditions and working environment;
- the right to just conditions of work and to fair remuneration including the right of women and men to equal pay for work of equal value;
- the right to vocational guidance and vocational training, the integration of disabled persons in the working world;
- prohibition of the employment of children under the age of fifteen and protection between fifteen and eighteen years of age;
- rights related to maternity;
- equal treatment for migrant workers.

b. *Social cohesion*

- The right to protection of health, the right to social security, the right to social and medical assistance and the right to benefit from social welfare services;
- the right of children and adolescents to protection against physical and moral dangers;
- the right of families and of their individual members to legal, social and economic protection;
- the right of migrant workers and their families to protection and assistance;
- the right of elderly persons to social protection.

At the time of ratification of the Charter, each state may decide to accept only a certain number of undertakings, with a minimum number of compulsory acceptances. Among these are at least five of the seven Articles considered to protect the most fundamental of human rights. The seven Articles, commonly known as the "hard core" Articles, are the right to work (Article 1), the right to organise (Article 5), the right to bargain collectively (Article 6), the right to social security (Article 12), the right to social and medical assistance (Article 13), the right of the family to social, legal and economical protection (Article 16) and the rights of migrant workers and their families (Article 19) (see Fact Sheet B – 2).

The system of supervision provided for in the Charter is based on reports submitted by Contracting Parties[1] (see Fact Sheet A – 5) and since the entry into force of the Protocol providing for a system of collective complaints on 1 July 1998, it is also carried out through the examination of collective complaints filed by social partners and certain NGOs to the European Committee of Social Rights (see Fact Sheets A – 13 and A – 14).

---

1. Contracting Party: state having ratified the Charter and bound by this instrument.

The European Social Charter and the Community Charter of the Fundamental Social Rights of Workers

1. The Social Charter and the Community Charter

The European Social Charter is a treaty which is binding on those states that have ratified it and which contains specific legal obligations for them (see Fact Sheet A – 1).

In contrast, the Community Charter of the Fundamental Social Rights of Workers is a political declaration containing no legal obligations: its implementation is provided for through other texts, such as European Union directives.

The Community Charter of the Fundamental Social Rights of Workers was adopted in Strasbourg on 9 December 1989 by the Heads of State and Government of eleven member states of the European Union: Belgium, Denmark, France, Germany, Greece, Ireland, Italy, Luxembourg, the Netherlands, Portugal and Spain (all member states of the European Community at that time, with the exception of the United Kingdom). Since that date, the three new member states (Austria, Finland and Sweden) and the United Kingdom have adopted the declaration.

The Community Charter, commonly known as the "Social Charter", is frequently confused with the Council of Europe's Social Charter, on which it is in fact based. The confusion is all the greater in that this text, a demonstration of the political will of the European Union's member states to promote the social aspects of the European Community, sets out a number of rights that should be guaranteed to all European citizens. These rights are in part identical to those effectively guaranteed by the Council of Europe's Social Charter. However, they mainly concern rights related to employment rather than those related to social cohesion which are less directly addressed (see Fact Sheet A – 1).

2. The fundamental social rights set out in the Community Charter

- free movement of workers;
- employment and wages (prohibition of forced labour, fair wages);
- improvement of living and working conditions;
- welfare protection;
- health and safety protection at work;
- protection of children and adolescents;
- protection of the elderly;
- protection of disabled persons.

3. Implementation of the Community Charter

Responsibility for enforcement of the rights laid down in the Community Charter lies with the member states and the European Commission, which prepares initiatives to ensure adoption of the directives and regulations required to implement these rights.

Several directives have thus been adopted:

- Directive 91/383 supplementing the measures to encourage improvements in the safety and health at work of workers with a fixed- duration employment relationship or a temporary employment relationship;
- Directive 91/933 on employers' obligation to inform workers of the conditions applicable to the employment contract or relationship;
- Directive 92/85 on the safety and health at work of pregnant workers and workers who have recently given birth or are breastfeeding;
- Directive 93/104 concerning certain aspects of the organization of working time;
- Directive 94/33 on the protection of young people at work;
- Directive 94/45 on the establishment of a European Works Council or a procedure in Community-scale undertakings and Community-scale groups of undertakings for the purposes of informing and consulting employees.

The Commission must also draw up an annual report on the Community Charter's application by the member states and the European Community. In practice, this system only functioned between 1990 and 1993, and has since been abandoned.

4. Scope of application

The Council of Europe's European Social Charter has a much wider field of application than the European Union charter. It guarantees social rights to the population as a whole (not only to workers).

5. The Council of Europe's Charter and the European Union

The European Social Charter of the Council of Europe has been ratified by the fifteen member states of the European Union and since the
entry into force of the Amsterdam Treaty on 1 May 1999 is directly
referred to in the Preamble and in Article 136 (former Article 117) of
the Treaty on the European Union.

Preamble:

*"(...) Confirming their attachment to fundamental social rights as
defined in the European Social Charter signed at Turin on 18 October
1961 and in the 1989 Community Charter of the Fundamental Social
Rights of Workers (...)"*

Article 136 – First paragraph:

*"The Community and the Member States, having in mind fundamental
social rights such as those set out in the European Social Charter signed
at Turin on 18 October 1961 and in the 1989 Community Charter of
the Fundamental Social Rights of Workers, shall have as their objectives
the promotion of employment, improved living and working conditions,
so as to make possible their harmonisation while the improvement is
being maintained, proper social protection, dialogue between management and labour, the development of human resources with a view to
lasting high employment and the combating of exclusion."*

The implementation of the new provisions of the Treaty on the
European Union will ensure a link between the legal systems of the
European Union and of the Council of Europe for the months and
years to come. The two treaties in combination will give European citizens the full benefit of all the fundamental rights of individuals.

The 1988 Additional Protocol

The 1988 Additional Protocol enlarged the scope *ratione materiae* of the 1961 Charter by adding rights divided into four new articles to the rights set out in the nineteen articles of the Charter.

These rights are:
- the right to equal opportunities and equal treatment in matters of employment and occupation without discrimination on the grounds of sex (Article 1);
- the right to information and consultation (Article 2);
- the right to take part in the determination and improvement of the working conditions and working environment (Article 3);
- the right of elderly persons to social protection (Article 4).

To date, the Protocol has been ratified by the Czech Republic, Denmark, Finland, Greece, the Netherlands, Norway, Slovakia and Spain. States that ratified the Protocol recently have submitted reports on the application of its provisions which were examined during supervision cycles XIII-3, XIII-5 and XIV-2 and XV-1.

The rights guaranteed by these articles have been included in the revised Social Charter of 1996; they correspond to Articles 20, 21, 22 and 23. As such, the Parties to the revised Charter have accepted them: Bulgaria, France, Italy, Romania, Slovenia and Sweden.

The 1988 Additional Protocol is therefore presently in force in fourteen countries.

The revised European Social Charter

During the 98th session of the Committee of Ministers, held on 3 May 1996, the revised European Social Charter was opened for signature. It has now been ratified by Bulgaria, France, Italy, Romania, Slovenia and Sweden, and has been signed by Albania, Austria, Belgium, Cyprus, Denmark, Estonia, Finland, Greece, Iceland, Lithuania, Luxembourg, Moldova, Portugal, Slovakia, Ukraine and the United Kingdom.

The revised Charter entered into force on 1 July 1999.

The text combines in a single instrument the rights guaranteed by the 1961 Charter with a certain number of amendments, plus the rights guaranteed by the Additional Protocol of 1988 and new rights.

1. List of amended provisions

Article 2 – The right to just conditions of work

The minimum length of paid holidays is raised from two weeks in the Charter to four weeks in the revised Charter.

Article 2 para. 4, which provides that workers engaged in dangerous or unhealthy occupations shall benefit from reduced working hours or additional paid holidays, has been amended to reflect the current trend towards eliminating the risks to which workers are exposed.

A new paragraph in this Article obliges the Parties to ensure that workers are informed of the essential aspects of their contract or employment relationship.

Another new paragraph provides that workers carrying out night work should benefit from measures which take into account the special nature of the work.

Article 3 – The right to safe and healthy working conditions

Through its new provisions, this Article obliges the Parties to define, implement and periodically review a coherent national policy on occupational safety, occupational health and the working environment. Article 3 para. 4 obliges the Parties to promote the progressive development of occupational health services, with essentially preventive and advisory functions.

Article 7 – *The right of children and young persons to protection*

The minimum age of admission to employment for prescribed occupations regarded as dangerous or unhealthy, which was not specified in the Charter, has now been set at eighteen.

The age up to which working hours must be restricted has been raised from sixteen in the Charter to eighteen in the revised Charter.

The minimum length of annual holiday with pay for workers aged under eighteen has been increased from three weeks in the Charter to four weeks in the revised Charter.

Article 8 – *The right of employed women to protection of maternity*

The length of maternity leave has been increased from twelve weeks in the Charter to fourteen weeks in the revised Charter.

Article 8 para. 2 of the revised Charter extends the period during which a pregnant woman may not be given notice of dismissal. This period now starts at the time she notifies her employer of her pregnancy and lasts until the end of her maternity leave.

In order to take into account the principle of equality between women and men, this Article has been amended so as to specifically protect employed women only in situations related to maternity. It requires that night work be regulated for women who are pregnant, have just given birth or who are breastfeeding and the prohibition of their employment in underground mining and in all other work which is dangerous, unhealthy or arduous.

Article 10 – *The right to vocational guidance*

A new paragraph 4, rendered necessary by the increase in long-term unemployment, had to be added to this Article; its aim is to provide or promote special measures for the retraining and reintegration of the long-term unemployed.

Article 12 – *The right to social security*

The second paragraph of Article 12 has been amended. It now refers to the European Code of Social Security and no longer to ILO Convention No. 102 concerning minimum standards of social security.

Article 15 – The right of persons with disabilities to independence, social integration and participation in the life of the community

In comparison with Article 15 of the Charter, the protection of persons with disabilities has been extended: the revised Charter no longer refers solely to vocational training and rehabilitation, but also lays down the right of persons with disabilities to individual social integration, personal independence and participation in the life of the community.

Article 17 – The right of children and young persons to social, legal and economic protection

The re-drafting of Article 17 in the revised Charter guarantees protection for children and young persons which goes beyond the context of employment and is intended to meet the specific needs stemming from their vulnerability. The provisions of this Article apply to all children, whether born in or out of wedlock. The protection provided by Article 17 of the Charter (right of mothers and children to social and economic protection) is covered by Article 16 of the revised Charter, to which an appendix has been added.

Article 19 – The right of migrant workers and their families to protection and assistance

In the Appendix to Article 9 para. 6, the definition of the "family of a foreign worker" has been modified. Firstly, it is no longer only the wife of a worker who is covered by this provision, but the spouse, male or female, of the worker. Secondly, the children admitted for family reunion are no longer dependent children under twenty-one years of age but dependent unmarried children for as long as they are considered as minors by the host country. Two new paragraphs have been added to Article 19: paragraph 11, the aim of which is to promote and facilitate the teaching of the national language of the receiving state to migrant workers and members of their families, and paragraph 12, which makes the same provisions in respect of the teaching of the migrant worker's mother tongue to his children.

2. The new rights set out in the revised Charter

The right to protection in cases of termination of employment (Article 24)

This Article protects workers from unfair dismissal: the workers have a right not to have their employment terminated without valid reasons. This right must cover the possibility of appeal and the granting of compensation.

The right of workers to the protection of their claims in the event of the insolvency of their employer (Article 25)

Under this Article, workers' claims arising from contracts of employment or employment relationships must be guaranteed by a guarantee institution or by any other effective form of protection.

The right to dignity at work (Article 26)

The revised Social Charter provides for measures to promote awareness, information and prevention measures in order to protect workers from sexual harassment or any other offensive action taken against them.

The right of workers with family responsibilities to equal opportunities and equal treatment (Article 27)

The aim of this Article is to prevent family responsibilities from diminishing workers' professional opportunities. It requires that specific measures be taken, in particular to facilitate remaining and re-entering employment after an absence, in relation to childcare arrangements and parental leave.

The right of workers' representatives to protection in undertakings and facilities to be accorded to them (Article 28)

Freedom of association is reinforced in the revised Charter: workers' representatives are specifically protected against any measure prejudicial to them based on their trade union membership. Furthermore, they must be afforded facilities allowing them to carry out their responsibilities efficiently.

The right to information and consultation in collective redundancy procedures (Article 29)

The right to information and consultation is already covered by Article 21. General in scope, this Article is supplemented in the revised Charter by Article 29 which concerns more specifically collective redundancy procedures.

The right to protection against poverty and social exclusion (Article 30)

Acute poverty and its dismantling effect on social cohesion is one the most serious threats to our contemporary societies. The revised Social Charter takes this new development into account and combats it by making the enforcement of a global and co-ordinated policy against social exclusion a requirement for Contracting Parties.

The right to housing (Article 31)

The right to housing is part of the plan of action to combat poverty and social exclusion. Article 31 provides for various measures to be taken, in particular in the field of access to housing.

In addition, the revised Charter includes provisions from the 1961 Charter which have been modified. These are, in particular:

– Article E, which is now a non-discrimination clause (along the lines of Article 14 of the European Convention on Human Rights); the reference to non-discrimination in the Charter appeared in the Preamble;

– Article J, which concerns the procedure for amendments: in the future, it will be possible to add new rights to the revised Charter.

Moreover, two new provisions, Articles 7 and 20, have been added to the Articles which make up the hard core of the revised Charter. Finally, the minimum number of hard core Articles which must be accepted has been raised to six (see Fact Sheets A – 1 and B – 2).

3. The supervisory machinery of the revised Charter

The supervisory machinery of the revised Charter is the same as that of the Charter: ie. one based on reports submitted by the Parties[1] and, for the states that have ratified the Additional Protocol to the Charter of 1995 or made the declaration provided for in Article D of the revised Charter, on a system of collective complaints.

---

1. Parties: states that have ratified the revised Charter and that are bound by this treaty.

The procedure for examining national reports and the 1991 Amending Protocol

Supervision of the implementation of the obligations contained in the Charter of 1961 (and in the revised Charter) is subject to international supervision based on national reports which the Contracting Parties submit at regular intervals (Article 21 of the 1961 Social Charter and Part IV, Article C of the revised Social Charter).

The reports are submitted according to the system described in the second part of this book (see Fact Sheet B – 7). The reference period is two years for the hard core provisions and four years for the other provisions.

The Protocol Amending the European Social Charter (known as the Turin Protocol) was adopted in 1991 in order to improve the supervisory system of the Social Charter. It will officially enter into force once all the Contracting Parties have ratified it. However, it has already been partially implemented following a decision by the Committee of Ministers in December 1991 asking the supervisory bodies to apply it before its entry into force to the extent that the text of the Charter permits.[1]

The Turin Protocol introduces the following changes:

– It clarifies the respective roles of the Governmental Committee and the European Committee of Social Rights, committee of independent experts of the Social Charter: according to Article 2 of the Protocol, only the European Committee of Social Rights is competent to determine from a legal standpoint the compliance of national law and practice with the obligations arising under the Charter.

---

1. In practice, all the provisions of the Amending Protocol are applied with the exception of the provision providing that the European Committee of Social Rights be elected by the Parliamentary Assembly (Article 3).

– It improves the procedure for consultation with NGOs and employer and trade union organisations: Contracting Parties must now send a copy of their reports to national organisations affiliated to international organisations of employers and trade unions that have observer status at the meetings of the Governmental Committee. Furthermore, a copy of the reports must also be sent to international NGOs with consultative status in the Council of Europe and who have particular competence in the matters governed by the Charter.

– By virtue of Article 6 of the Amending Protocol, the Parliamentary Assembly is no longer a supervisory body. It is, however, still associated in the supervisory process in that it uses the conclusions of the European Committee of Social Rights as a basis for its periodic debates on social policy.

– It has specified the procedure for adopting individual recommendations by modifying the majority required for their adoption by the Committee of Ministers: two thirds of Contracting Parties to the Charter and not two thirds of member states of the Council of Europe must vote in favour of the recommendation in order for it to be adopted.

The following supervisory bodies are involved in the supervision procedure:[1]

– the European Committee of Social Rights, committee of independent experts of the Charter (see also Fact Sheet A – 7), composed of nine experts elected by the Committee of Ministers and assisted by an International Labour Organisation observer. It examines reports submitted by the Contracting Parties and gives a legal assessment of these states' fulfilment of their undertakings;

– the Governmental Committee (see also Fact Sheet A – 8), composed of representatives of the Contracting Parties to the Charter and assisted by observers from European labour and management organisations. It prepares the decisions of the Committee of Ministers and, in particular, selects, on the basis of social, economic and other policy considerations, the situations which should be the subject of recommendations to each Contracting Party;

– the Committee of Ministers (see also Fact Sheet A – 9), which adopts a resolution for the supervision cycle as a whole and issues recommendations (see Fact Sheet A – 10) asking states to amend their legislation and practice in order to comply with the Charter.

---

1. See also the table opposite.

European Social Charter

Supervisory mechanism

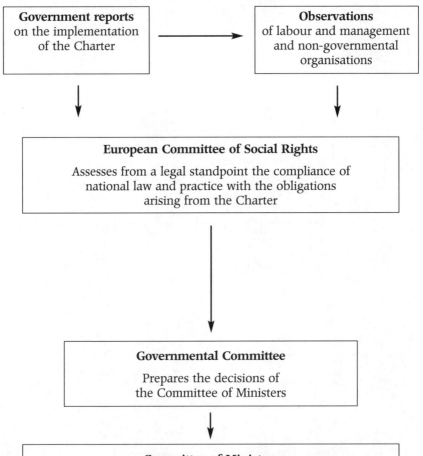

The Article 22 procedure (non-accepted provisions)

As Article 20 of the European Social Charter makes clear, Contracting Parties are not obliged to accept the totality of its provisions as long as they accept a minimum number of undertakings from both the hard core and non-hard core Articles. To date, only three states (Belgium, the Netherlands and Portugal) have accepted all the Charter's provisions and one state (France) has done so for the revised Charter. Parties may of course decide to accept further undertakings at a later date, but this is unusual. In this context, the procedure for reporting on provisions of the Charter which have not been accepted (Article 22) acquires a special significance.

Pursuant to Article 22, the Committee of Ministers may request states to report on Charter provisions they have not yet accepted. To date, this procedure has been followed on six occasions. Reports are transmitted to the European Committee of Social Rights, which examines states' reasons for deciding not to accept the provisions in question. A short report is then published containing the Committee's observations.

In each of its reports on non-accepted provisions, the Committee underlines the usefulness of the Article 22 procedure. It provides the opportunity to obtain a clearer picture of how the various standards contained in the Charter are implemented in the Contracting Parties, even where they have been not been formally accepted. The Committee's comments provide indicators to states as to the steps they should take in order to accept a given provision. Under Article 23 of the Charter, states are obliged to communicate their reports to certain national employers' and trade union organisations, which may make comments (see Fact Sheet B – 8).

In the **first Article 22 exercise,** states were asked to report on Articles 4 para. 3 (equal pay for men and women), 7 para. 1 (prohibition of the employment of children under fifteen years of age), 8 para.1 (paid maternity leave) and 8 para. 2 (prohibition of dismissal during maternity leave). Since the publication of that report (in 1981), Cyprus has accepted Articles 7 para. 1 and 8 paras. 1 and 2.

The **second exercise** concerned Articles 2 para. 4 (extra holidays or reduced working time in prescribed dangerous or unhealthy occupations), 7 para. 4 (limited working hours for young persons under sixteen), 8 para. 4 (regulation of night work for women in industry and the prohibition on women's mining work and other dangerous occupations) and 19 para. 8 (protection of migrant workers against expulsion). Since publication of the report in 1982, France has accepted Article 2 para. 4.

The **third exercise** covered Articles 2 para. 1 (reasonable daily and weekly working hours), 7 paras. 5, 6 and 7 (providing protection in a number of areas for young workers). Since the report was published in 1989, Cyprus has accepted Articles 2 para. 1 and 7 para. 7.

The **fourth exercise** under Article 22 covered Articles 7 para. 9 (regular medical control of young workers in certain prescribed occupations) and 19 para. 4 (equal treatment between nationals and migrant workers in certain areas). The Committee's report was published in 1995.

The **fifth exercise** under Article 22 concerned Article 4 para. 4 (reasonable notice of dismissal). The report was published in 1997.

Finally, the **sixth exercise** covered Articles 5 (the right to organise) and 6 (the right to bargain collectively) for states which have not accepted all the provisions of these Articles. The Committee's report was published in 1998.

The seventh exercise will cover Articles 5, 6 and 13 and the eighth will cover Articles 3, 4 and 7.

Once the European Committee of Social Rights' reports are published, they are submitted to the Governmental Committee, then to the Committee of Ministers, which closes the procedure with the adoption of a resolution.

The European Committee of Social Rights

1. Composition

The members of the European Committee of Social Rights, committee of independent experts established under Article 25 of the European Social Charter, are elected by the Committee of Ministers of the Council of Europe. When the Committee was created, the Committee of Ministers fixed membership at seven.

The 1991 Amending Protocol modified Article 25 of the Charter by providing that the Committee should be composed of at least nine members, the exact number to be fixed by the Committee of Ministers. Following the decision of the Committee of Ministers to apply the Amending Protocol before its entry into force to the extent the text of the Charter permits, the decision was taken during the course of the 509th meeting of the delegates in March 1994 to increase from seven to nine the number of members of the Committee.

In order to accommodate the increase in the number of Contracting Parties to the Charter and ensure the participation of specialists from different European legal systems, a further increase in membership of the Committee, from nine to twelve and later fifteen, is under consideration. The procedure for the enlargement is currently being discussed.

The Committee of Social Rights holds eight weekly sessions per year. In order to rationalise the examination of the reports submitted to it the Committee has formed two working groups (one composed of five experts and the other composed of four experts) that prepares its decisions.

The members of the Committee are appointed for six years. This mandate is renewable once.

At 1 January 2000, the Committee was composed as follows:

Mr Matti MIKKOLA, President
Professor of Labour Law at the Universities of Helsinki and Talinn
Finnish

Mr Rolf BIRK, First Vice-President
Professor, Director of the Institute of Labour Law and Industrial
Relations in the EEC at the University of Trier
German

Mr Stein EVJU, Second Vice-President
President of the Labour Court of Norway and Professor of Labour Law
at the University of Oslo
Norwegian

Ms Suzanne GRÉVISSE, General Rapporteur
Honorary Chairman of the Social Department of the Conseil d'Etat
French

Mr Konrad GRILLBERGER
Professor, Director of the Institute of Labour Law and Social
Legislation at the University of Salzburg
Austrian

Mr Alfredo BRUTO DA COSTA
Assistant Professor at the Portuguese Catholic University of Lisbon
Portuguese

Mrs Micheline JAMOULLE
Professor at the Law Faculty of the University of Liège
Belgian

Mr Nikitas ALIPRANTIS
Professor at the Democritos University of Thrace and at the University
Robert Schuman of Strasbourg
Greek

Mr Tekin AKILLIOĞLU
Professor of Public Law and Director of the Human Rights Centre of
the University of Ankara
Turkish

In addition, Ms Jacqueline ANCEL-LENNERS represents the International Labour Office and participates as a consultant in the Committee's deliberations.

2. Functions

The European Committee of Social Rights assesses the compliance of Contracting Parties with their obligations. Assessment takes the form of conclusions: a conclusion is positive if the Committee finds the situation to be in conformity with the Charter and negative if the situation is not in conformity with the Charter. Where the Committee does not have the necessary information to assess the situation, the conclusion is deferred until the next supervision cycle.

In the course of its examination of national reports, the Committee may hold meetings with representatives of the Contracting Parties. The social partners are invited to participate in these meetings.

Under the Additional Protocol of 1995, the Committee is also the supervisory body to which collective complaints are submitted: by virtue of Article 6 and 7 of the Collective Complaints Protocol the Committee is competent to decide on the admissibility of complaints and to draw up a report containing its conclusions as to whether or not the situation is in conformity with the Charter. During its examination, the Committee may hold a hearing between the parties to the complaint.

The Governmental Committee

1. Composition

By virtue of Article 27 of the Social Charter, the Governmental Committee of the Charter is composed of representatives of all the Contracting Parties. Observers from two international organisations of employers and from two international trade unions are invited, in an advisory capacity, to attend the meetings. The Governmental Committee may further consult up to two representatives of international non- governmental organisations with consultative status in the Council of Europe on questions the organisations are particularly qualified to deal with, such as social welfare and the social and economic protection of the family.

It should also be noted that in view of preparing for ratification of the European Social Charter by the member states of eastern and central Europe, the Committee of Ministers decided, in October 1992, to invite those having signed the Charter to meetings of the Governmental Committee as observers. To date, the following countries have either participated in these meetings as observers before their ratification of the Charter or are still attending as signatory states: Albania, Bulgaria, Croatia, the Czech Republic, Estonia, Hungry, Latvia, Lithuania, Moldova, Romania, Slovenia, "the former Yugoslav Republic of Macedonia" and Ukraine.

In December 1998 this invitation was extended to all signatory states, and therefore now includes Switzerland and Liechtenstein.

2. Functions

The Governmental Committee's role as defined in Article 27 para. 3 is to prepare a report for the Committee of Ministers in which it selects, from the national situations which the European Committee of Social Rights has found to be in breach of the Charter, those which should be the subject of recommendations.

3. **Working methods of the Committee**

A. *Mandate of the Committee*

The Committee, following the request made in the final resolution of the Ministerial Conference in Turin and in the decision of the Committee of Ministers of 11 December 1991 that the supervisory bodies apply the Amending Protocol as far as possible before its entry into force, refrains from the formulation of legal interpretations of the provisions of the Charter and assumes the responsibilities foreseen in Article 4 of the Amending Protocol. The provision in question reads as follows:

> *"Article 4*
>
> *3. The Governmental Committee shall prepare the decisions of the Committee of Ministers. In particular, in the light of the reports of the Committee of Independent Experts and of the Contracting Parties, it shall select, giving reasons for its choice, on the basis of social, economic and other policy considerations the situations which should, in its view, be the subject of recommendations to each Contracting Party concerned, in accordance with Article 28 of the Charter. It shall present to the Committee of Ministers a report which shall be made public.*
>
> *4. On the basis of its findings on the implementation of the Social Charter in general, the Governmental Committee may submit proposals to the Committee of Ministers aiming at studies to be carried out on social issues and on articles of the Charter which possibly might be updated."*

B. *General observations on the national reports and on the Conclusions of the European Committee of Social Rights*

The Committee comments on the national reports and on the conclusions of the European Committee of Social Rights, and in particular on the general introduction to the Conclusions. The Committee drafts an introduction in which it indicates the developments since the previous cycle of supervision and, if need be, its suggestions on the application of Article 4 para. 4 of the Amending Protocol.

C. *Examination of negative conclusions:*

I. *Procedure*

The Committee:

- considers the conclusions provision by provision;
- takes a vote in respect of each negative conclusion of the European Committee of Social Rights, unless there is a consensus not to take a vote; the first vote will be on whether to suggest that a recommendation be addressed to the state concerned. Regarding recommendations, the Committee decides to respect the same voting rules as those of the Committee of Ministers (two-thirds majority of votes cast and simple majority of Contracting Parties);

– where there is no majority in favour of a recommendation, it will then also take a vote on whether to address a warning to the state concerned (two-thirds majority of votes cast). If a warning follows a negative conclusion, it serves as an indication to the state that, unless it takes measures to comply with its obligations under the Charter, a recommendation will be proposed in the next part of a cycle where this provision is under examination;

– where neither a recommendation nor a warning is proposed, the Committee may find it necessary to express an opinion on the national situation or on the conclusion of the European Committee of Social Rights in its report to the Committee of Ministers;

– the Committee's vote on a national situation will be final unless a delegate expressly requests a further vote at the end of the part of the cycle;

– in so far as the examination concerns a Contracting Party submitting its first report, the subject of the first set of conclusions of the European Committee of Social Rights, the Committee issues a warning rather than a recommendation in the case of negative conclusions. The Committee considers this approach necessary in order to give the countries concerned some time to consider and respond to the findings of the Committee of Social Rights.

II. Selection criteria:

a. Does the provision in question belong to the hard core of the Charter or of the revised Charter?

b. Is the provision among those which have been updated by the revised Social Charter?

c. Since which cycle has the situation been criticised?

d. Is there a significant number of persons not protected and what are the consequences of non-compliance for those involved?

e. How serious does the European Committee of Social Rights consider the situation to be?

f. Has the Parliamentary Assembly expressed an opinion during its periodical debates on the Charter as to the importance of the protection guaranteed by the provision in question?

g. Have the social partners expressed an opinion on the seriousness of this type of breach?

h. What was the Governmental Committee's position in response to the previous conclusion of the European Committee of Social Rights on this point? Was a recommendation adopted by the Committee of Ministers?

i. Is the country taking or planning to take measures to modify the criticised situation?

j. Does the criticised situation also concern another provision of the Charter?

    k. What was the decision of the Committee in similar situations?

  D. *Examination of adjournments for lack of information*

    I. Procedure

The Committee:

- no longer examines during sessions the national situations having been the object of an adjourned conclusion following a question asked by the European Committee of Social Rights for the first time except if a delegation calls for such an examination; these situations will nevertheless be referred to in the working document and in the report to the Committee of Ministers, as a reminder. The delegates concerned can, however, transmit written information to the Secretariat which they would like to be included in the Committee's reports.

- takes a vote on each situation in which the European Committee of Social Rights has repeatedly had to defer a conclusion for lack of information; a warning is adopted with a two-thirds majority of votes cast; a warning in respect of an adjourned conclusion will be made in cases of repeated lack of information, as an encouragement to submit all the relevant information in the next report. Here again, the state will be informed that if the information is not submitted, a proposal for a recommendation will follow in the next cycle.

    II. Selection criteria:

    a. Cycle since which the European Committee of Social Rights has found it impossible to take a conclusion because of lack of information;

    b. whether the Governmental Committee has issued a warning or proposed a recommendation and whether a recommendation was adopted;

    c. practical reasons given by the state concerned to explain its failure to respond;

    d. failure to submit reports and information requested within the time limit;

    e. failure to submit reports to the social partners and comments made by social partners.

  E. *Report to the Committee of Ministers*

The report indicates developments since the previous supervision cycle, showing positive and negative changes in the national situations.

It contains, *inter alia,* general observations on the measures taken by the different states to comply with recommendations made by the Committee of Ministers, as well as the proposals for individual recommendations to be addressed to the states by the Committee of Ministers.

Only the proposals for first recommendations are appended to the draft resolution; the renewal of recommendations still to be acted upon is mentioned only in the draft resolution ending the supervision cycle.

F. *Follow-up of individual recommendations*

Contracting Parties shall report on the measures taken to comply with the recommendations made by the Committee of Ministers.

The Governmental Committee has a subsidiary role in the procedure for the examination of collective complaints: it is only consulted by the Committee of Ministers where the Contracting Party has explicitly requested that the Governmental Committee be consulted, where the report of the Committee of Social Rights raises new issues and where a two-thirds majority of the Contracting Parties to the Charter are in favour of such consultation.

The Committee of Ministers

1. Composition

The Committee of Ministers is made up of one representative – the Minister for Foreign Affairs – of each of the Council of Europe's member states. "When a Minister for Foreign Affairs is unable to be present or in other circumstances where it may be desirable, an alternate may be nominated to act for him, who shall, whenever possible, be a member of his government".[1] A minister may be represented by an alternate, be it another member of the government (a minister or secretary of state for European affairs, for example) or a high-ranking diplomat.

2. Functions

I. The Committee of Ministers, supervisory body of the Charter

The Committee of Ministers intervenes in the last stage of the supervisory process, both in the procedure based on national reports and the collective complaints procedure.

II. Reports

In the supervisory process based on national reports the Committee of Ministers, after receiving the report of the Governmental Committee to which the conclusions of the European Committee of Social Rights are attached, adopts a resolution closing each supervision cycle and addresses individual recommendations to Contracting Parties where necessary.

---

1. Statute of the Council of Europe (European Treaty Series ETS No. 1) Article 14. See also Rules of Procedure of the Committee of Ministers, Article 10.

A recommendation of the Committee of Ministers is now adopted by a two-thirds majority of those voting[1] and no longer by a majority of Council of Europe member states. Only Contracting Parties to the Charter may vote and not, as previously, all member states of the Council of Europe.[2]

Both decisions on the above-mentioned voting methods have allowed the political standpoint of the Committee of Ministers to be strengthened. Since 1993 (twelfth supervision cycle) the Committee of Ministers has made use of the possibility given to it to make recommendations. Although these recommendations do not have binding legal force, they have provided the supervisory mechanism of the Charter with a political means of sanctioning countries, which in some cases has prompted them to change legislation in order to bring it into conformity with the requirements of the Charter (see Fact Sheet A – 10 for a list of the recommendations addressed to Contracting Parties to date).

III. Collective complaints

The Committee of Ministers also plays a role in the last stage of the collective complaints procedure. Article 9 of the Protocol providing for a system of collective complaints provides that the Committee of Ministers shall adopt a resolution closing the procedure and, where appropriate it shall address a recommendation to the Contracting Party concerned in the event that the European Committee of Social Rights has found a breach of the Charter.

---

1. Decision on the adoption of recommendations under the European Social Charter, adopted by the Committee of Ministers at the 541st meeting of the Ministers' Deputies, 19-22 June 1995:
   The Deputies specified that following their decision, adopted at the 492nd meeting (April 1993, item 15) whereby "only the Representatives of those States which have ratified the Charter vote in the Committee of Ministers when the latter acts as a control organ of the application of the Charter," Recommendations under the European Social Charter are adopted by a majority of two-thirds of the Deputies casting a vote and a majority of the Contracting Parties to the Charter, (Article 9, paragraph 4 taken together with Article 10, paragraph 3 of the Rules of Procedure for the meetings of the Deputies).

2. Decision on voting in the Committee of Ministers, adopted by the Committee of Ministers in April 1993 at the 492nd meeting of the Ministers' Deputies:
   The Deputies,
   1. Agreed unanimously to the introduction of the rule whereby only the Representatives of those states which have ratified the Charter vote in the Committee of Ministers when the latter acts as a control organ of the Charter.

Recommendations adopted by the Committee of Ministers

Article 29 of the Charter provides that the Committee of Ministers of the Council of Europe may make any necessary recommendations to the Contracting Parties. The first time this procedure was used was at the end of supervision cycle XII-1. The Committee of Ministers recalled that the Amending Protocol to the Charter provided for the selection, by the Governmental Committee, of situations which, in light of social, economic and other policy considerations, should be the subject of recommendations to each Contracting Party. To date, the Committee of Ministers has adopted twenty-three recommendations, which have been addressed to thirteen Contracting Parties. The substance of each recommendation is indicated below. The full texts are to be found on the website: http://www.socialcharter.coe.int.

1. **Supervision cycle XII-1** (recommendations adopted on 7 September 1993)

   Greece

   Article 1 para. 2: forced labour – merchant navy, armed forces

   Article 13 para. 1: no individual right to social assistance

   Article 13 para. 4: discrimination against non-nationals

   Norway

   Article 6 para. 4: unjustified arbitration used in nurses' strike

   Article 7 para. 3: possibility of an unduly long working week for schoolchildren

   United Kingdom

   Article 6 para. 4: possibility of dismissal of strikers and selective re-hiring

   Article 8 para. 1: inadequate maternity benefits

2. Supervision cycle XII-2 (recommendations adopted on 8 April 1994)

Austria

Article 5:	no protection against dismissal on grounds of trade union activities in firms with less than 5 employees
Article 8 para. 2:	possibility of dismissing domestic employees after fifth month of pregnancy

Germany

Article 19 para. 6:	various restrictions on family reunion

France

Article 1 para. 2:	forced labour – merchant navy

Italy

Article 1 para. 2:	forced labour – merchant navy, civil aviation
Article 3 para. 2:	failure to provide necessary information for an assessment of the situation
Article 4 para. 4:	inadequate periods of notice of dismissal in certain sectors
Article 4 para. 5:	no regulation of wage deductions
Article 7 para. 1:	no prohibition on work of young persons under fifteen in agriculture and domestic work
Article 8 para. 1:	no paid maternity leave for domestic workers
Article 8 para. 2:	possibility of dismissal of domestic workers during maternity leave
Article 8 para. 3:	no entitlement to paid nursing breaks for domestic employees and home workers
Article 13 para. 1:	no individual right to social assistance

3. Supervision cycle XIII-1 (recommendations adopted on 22 May 1995)

Austria

Article 5:	no protection against dismissal on grounds of trade union activities in firms with less than five employees
Article 8 para. 2:	possibility of dismissing domestic employees after fifth month of pregnancy

Denmark

Article 5:	restrictions on right of association under Danish International Ships' Register
Article 6 para. 2:	restrictions on collective bargaining, and unequal treatment under Danish International Ships' Register

Article 6 para. 4: no right to strike for civil servants

France

Article 1 para. 2: forced labour – merchant navy

Greece

Article 1 para. 2: forced labour – merchant navy, armed forces

Article 7 para. 1: no minimum age for employment in agricultural, forestry or livestock work in family undertakings

Article 7 para. 3: no minimum age for employment in agricultural, forestry or livestock work in family undertakings

Article 19 para. 1: failure to provide necessary information for an assessment of the situation

Article 19 para. 8: no right of appeal against a deportation order

Ireland

Article 1 para. 2: forced labour, merchant navy

Article 4 para. 4: inadequate periods of notice of termination of employment

Article 6 para. 4: insufficient protection for merchant seamen on strike

Article 7 para. 3: insufficient regulation of working hours for children in the employment of a relative

Article 19 para. 8: no right of appeal against a deportation order

Italy

Article 1 para. 2: forced labour – merchant navy, civil aviation

Article 3 para. 1: certain self-employed workers without protection in matters of health and safety

Article 3 para. 2: certain self-employed workers without protection in matters of health and safety

Article 3 para. 2: failure to provide necessary information for an assessment of the situation

Article 4 para. 4: inadequate periods of notice of dismissal in certain sectors

Article 4 para. 5: no regulation of wage deductions

Spain

Article 1 para. 2: forced labour – merchant navy and aviation crew

Sweden

Article 19 para. 8: no right of appeal against deportation order

4. Supervision cycle XIII-2 (recommendations adopted on 14 December 1995)

Greece

Article 18 para. 2: failure to simplify procedures in respect of non-EU/EEA migrants

Italy

Article 7 para. 4: inadequate regulation of working hours for persons under 16 years of age

5. Supervision cycle XIII-3 (recommendations adopted on 15 January 1997)

Malta

Articles 5 and 6 para. 2: obligation on police to join Maltese Police Association. Impossibility of their affiliating with another union or association

Turkey

Article 7 para. 3: certain sectors not subject to prohibition on child labour

United Kingdom

Article 1 para. 2: forced labour – merchant navy

Articles 5 and 6 para. 2: legislative restrictions on freedom of association and collective bargaining

Articles 6 para. 4: possibility of dismissal of strikers and selective re-hiring

6. Supervision cycle XIII-4 (recommendations adopted on 4 February 1998)

France

Article 17: Inequality of inheritance rights for children born in adultery

Germany

Article 6 para. 4: restriction on the right to strike

Italy

Article 7 para. 2: minimum age too low for certain dangerous occupations (benzene)

Turkey

Article 11:   excessive infant and childbirth death rate

Article 16:   inequalities between parents and low proportion of families benefiting from family allowances

7. Supervision cycle XIII-5 (recommendations adopted on 2 July 1998)

Portugal

Article 7 par. 1:   no practical compliance with the prohibition of work for children under fifteen

8. Supervision cycle XIV-1 (recommendations adopted on 4 March 1999)

Austria

Article 5:   election to works councils restricted to nationals

Ireland

Article 5
and 6 par.2:   legislative restrictions on freedom of association and collective bargaining

9. Supervision cycle XIV-2 (recommendations adopted on 27 October 1999)

Turkey

Article 4 para. 3: no prohibition of wage discrimination between women and men in certain sectors of the economy

Main points of Conclusions XIV-1 and XIV-2

1. Conclusions XIV-1

The conclusions for supervision cycle XIV-1, concerned Articles 1, 5, 6, 12, 13, 16 and 19 of the Charter. The reference period was 1994-96. The Committee's conclusions are presented for the first time country by country, rather than provision by provision. The aim of this change is to make it easier for readers to verify their country's compliance with the Charter. Special attention should also be paid to the general introduction to the Conclusions which, as in the past, reviews the principal themes and stresses the essential elements underlying each provision of the Charter under consideration.

In relation to **Article 1** (the right to work), the Committee noted that the number of unemployed persons in the Contracting Parties stood at between 22 and 23 millions during the reference period. Although it does not reach conclusions on compliance of national situations with Article 1 para. 1, the Committee examines all developments and initiatives in the employment field. It noted that serious problems of discrimination in employment persist, even if the de jure situation in most states is satisfactory. Concerning forced labour, the Committee insisted that recommendations to the many states still failing to respect the Charter provisions be worded more firmly.

With respect to **Articles 5 and 6** (the right to organise and to bargain collectively), the Committee highlighted the importance of these provisions and urged all states to accept them, since they are instrumental in complying with the rest of the Charter. Both Articles were the subject of the sixth Article 22 report on unaccepted provisions. The Committee posed general questions to states on trade union representativity rules and restrictions on the eligibility of non-national trade union delegates for official tri-partite bodies.

Aware of the important developments which have occurred in the field of social security (**Article 12**), the Committee recalled that adjustments may be made to social security systems on social and economic grounds, but that the level of protection must be maintained and the means chosen must be appropriate. It has also reminded states of the duty to treat non-nationals equally and to ensure the granting, maintenance and resumption of social security rights wherever the persons concerned move within the territories of the Contracting Parties.

Concerning the right to social and medical assistance (**Article 13**), the Committee again emphasised that the Charter confers an individual right on all persons in need of adequate assistance. States are, moreover, under an obligation to work towards the elimination of poverty, making social assistance eventually unnecessary.

Under **Article 16** (protection of the family), the Committee again criticised the requirement of residence for a child within the national territory before child benefit is payable. The Charter does not prohibit a reduction in the level of benefit if the country in which the child resides has a lower cost of living, provided that the reduction is proportional. Similarly, the Committee stated that if a length of residence requirement for the payment of child benefit is admissible under Article 12 para. 4, it will also be acceptable under Article 16.

Lastly, under **Article 19** (rights of migrant workers), the Committee pointed to the serious problems still facing migrant workers: discrimination, restrictions on family reunion and deportation arrangements which do not meet the Charter's criteria.

A total of 489 situations were reported on by the Contracting Parties. In more than half of these (281), the Committee was satisfied that the Charter was being fully implemented. Negative conclusions were reached in respect of 100 situations.

2. Conclusions XIV-2

The conclusions for supervision cycle XIV-2 concerned Articles 2, 3, 9, 10, and 15 of the Charter and Articles 2 and 3 of the Additional Protocol of 1988 for states that have ratified it. The reference period was 1992-1996.

Under **Article 2**, the Committee stressed that working hours, including overtime, should be reasonable so as not to jeopardise the health and safety of the workers concerned. It found, for instance, that a possibility in national legislation of working up to sixteen hours in a single twenty-four hour period was not in conformity with the Charter. It also noted the increasing use of flexible working time schemes in many Contracting Parties, notably based on the averaging of working hours over periods longer than the working week. The Committee has considered that these systems are not as such in breach of the Charter. However, the special conditions for establishing these systems and limits to working time must be observed.

With respect to **Article 3**, the Committee examined regulations on risks connected with certain activities (eg. fishing, dock work, construction and mining), and with hazardous substances and agents (notably asbestos and ionising radiation), as well as on risks encountered by certain vulnerable categories of workers. Generally, it found the development in trends of industrial accidents, including fatal accidents, and as regards the supervisory activities of the national labour inspectorates, to be satisfactory, although problems remained in certain Contracting Parties.

As regards the right to a fair remuneration laid down in **Article 4,** the Committee confirmed the basic principle that the minimum wage in the labour market (whether determined by statute or by practice after negotiation) should not be lower than the average wage. It has decided, however, to modify its assessment method and will henceforth look at net wages of full-time workers, ie. after deduction of social contributions and taxes. It fixed the limit below which a net wage cannot be considered fair within the meaning of the Charter at 60% of the net national average wage.

Assessing the commitment of states to ensure the effective exercise of the right to vocational guidance in **Article 9,** the Committee highlighted the resources invested, both human and financial, the efficiency of information dissemination and the principle of equal treatment of nationals of other Contracting Parties in guidance provision.

In relation to **Article 10,** the Committee noted the efforts made by governments to meet the socio-economic and technological challenges to the national vocational training systems. It assessed the sufficiency of these efforts in the light of the Charter's requirements, inter alia, by looking at spending on training, on participation and availability of training places. It nevertheless observed that equal treatment for nationals of the other Contracting Parties in access to training and in particular to financial assistance is still not ensured in a number of states.

The aim of **Article 15** is to ensure the effective exercise of the right of physically or mentally disabled persons to vocational training, rehabilitation and resettlement. The Committee observed the priority given in most states to integrating disabled persons into the ordinary training and working environment, but nevertheless warned against the risk of marginalising disabled persons in specialised institutions. Also under this provision problems of equal treatment in law and in practice of nationals of other Contracting Parties persist in certain states.

Supervision of the application of the European Social Charter: situation at the end of cycle XIV-2

The following table summarises the country-by-country legal evaluation made by the European Committee of Social Rights on the conformity of national situations with the European Social Charter. It is based on the latest conclusions of the European Committee of Social Rights (Conclusions XIV-1 and XIV-2) for each provision of the Charter.

Key

+	Positive conclusion
(+)	Provisionally positive conclusion
–	Negative conclusion
0	Deferral
black	Provisions not accepted
grey	Non hard-core provisions: Articles 2, 3, 4, 9, 10 and 15, plus Articles 2 and 3 of the Additional Protocol (except full reports from Italy and Norway). Conclusions XIV-2, published in December 1998. Next examination in cycle XVI-2 (Conclusions to be published in December 2002).
light grey	Hard core provisions examined during cycle XIV-1 (except Article 1.4 which was examined in cycle XIV-2): Articles 1, 5, 6, 12, 13, 16 and 19. Conclusions published in May 1998. Next examination in cycle XV-1 (Conclusions in April 2000).
white	Non hard-core provisions: Articles 7, 8, 11, 14, 17 and 18, plus Articles 1 and 4 of the Additional Protocol. Next examination in cycle XV-2 (Conclusions to be published in December 2000).

The Committee has not adopted conclusions under Article 1. 1 since the eighth supervision cycle.

Some provisions are the subject of two conclusions:

Article 1.2: elimination of all forms of discrimination in employment (ED) and prohibition of forced labour (FL);

Article 8.1: right to maternity leave (ML) and right to adequate benefits (AB);

Article 8.4: regulation of night work in industrial employment (NW) and prohibition of employment in dangerous tasks (DT).

	AU	BE	CY	DE	FI	FR	GE	GR	IC	IRL	IT	LU	MA	NL	NO	PO	SP	SW	TU	UK
1.1																				
1.2 ED	O	+	O	+	+	+	(+)	O	+	(+)	O	(+)	(+)	+	(+)	-	O	+	O	-
1.2 FL	+	-	-	-	+	-	+	-	+	-	-	(+)	(+)	-	+	-	+	+	-	-
1.3	+	O	+	(+)	(+)	+	+	-	O	(+)	(+)	(+)	O	+	+	+	(+)	+	-	+
1.4	-	-	+	O	O	+	+	O	O	O	O	O	O	+	+	O	+	+	-	+
2.1	■	-	O	■	-	+	O	-	-	O	O	O	O	-	-	+	-	■	■	■
2.2	+	+	■	+	+	+	+	O	■	+	+	+	+	+	+	-	+	■	■	+
2.3	+	+	+	+	+	+	+	+	+	+	O	+	-	+	+	+	+	+	■	O
2.4	O	-	■	■	+	+	+	O	■	-	-	-	■	-	+	O	O	■	■	O
2.5	+	+	+	+	O	+	+	+	+	O	+	O	+	O	+	+	O	+	■	O
3.1	+	+	+	+	■	O	+	O	O	+	-	O	O	-	+	+	O	+	■	+
3.2	O	O	+	+	■	+	+	O	O	O	O	O	O	O	+	-	O	+	■	+
3.3	+	+	+	+	+	+	+	+	+	+	+	+	+	O	+	+	+	+	■	+
4.1	O	O	■	O	■	O	O	O	O	-	O	O	O	O	O	O	-	O	■	-
4.2	+	-	■	+	O	+	O	O	+	+	+	O	+	+	+	+	-	+	-	-
4.3	■	+	■	+	O	+	■	O	O	■	O	■	O	+	O	O	O	■	■	■
4.4	■	-	■	■	O	-	■	-	O	-	-	■	-	-	+	O	-	-	■	-
4.5	+	+	■	■	O	+	■	+	+	O	-	O	O	+	+	+	+	■	O	O

	5	6.1	6.2	6.3	6.4	7.1	7.2	7.3	7.4	7.5	7.6	7.7	7.8	7.9	7.10	8.1ML	8.1AB	8.2
UK	-	o	-	+	-	■	+	-	■	o	(+)	■	■	+	+	-	-	■
TU	■	■	■	■	■	■	-	-	o	o	■	-	-	■	■	■	■	■
SW	-	+	+	+	(+)	-	+	-	+	■	■	+	+	o	+	-	+	■
SP	+	+	o	(+)	(+)	-	+	-	-	-	-	+	o	-	(+)	(+)	(+)	-
PO	o	(+)	o	o	-	-	o	-	o	o	(+)	+	-	+	+	-	+	+
NO	(+)	+	(+)	-	-	■	+	-	■	o	o	+	o	■	+	■	■	■
NL	+	+	(+)	+	(+)	+	+	-	(+)	-	-	+	+	+	(+)	-	-	(+)
MA	-	(+)	-	-	o	(+)	o	(+)	+	o	+	+	-	o	(+)	-	-	-
LU	-	+	+	+	■	+	o	+	-	-	o	+	+	(+)	+	+	+	-
IT	+	+	+	+	o	-	-	-	-	o	+	+	+	+	(+)	+	-	-
IRL	-	o	-	+	-	■	+	-	-	-	+	■	(+)	■	+	-	-	■
IC	-	+	+	+	-	■	■	■	■	■	■	■	■	■	■	■	■	■
GR	■	■	■	■	■	-	+	-	o	+	+	+	o	+	+	o	o	-
GE	(+)	+	(+)	+	■	■	+	(+)	+	o	+	+	+	+	+	(+)	■	■
FR	o	+	o	+	-	-	+	-	+	+	+	+	+	+	+	+	+	(+)
FI	o	(+)	(+)	+	o	o	o	-	o	+	■	+	+	■	+	■	■	o
DE	-	+	-	(+)	-	■	■	■	■	■	■	■	■	■	■	-	o	■
CY	+	+	(+)	+	o	(+)	■	(+)	■	■	■	+	-	■	■	+	o	(+)
BE	o	+	o	+	o	o	+	+	o	o	(+)	o	o	+	o	+	+	o
AU	-	+	+	+	■	+	-	+	+	■	+	+	+	(+)	+	+	-	-

	AU	BE	CY	DE	FI	FR	GE	GR	IC	IRL	IT	LU	MA	NL	NO	PO	SP	SW	TU	UK
8.3	+	-	■	■	■	0	(+)	+	■	■	-	+	■	-	■	+	+	-	■	■
8.4NW	+	0	■	■	■	0	■	0	■	-	0	■	0	+	■	0	+	■	■	■
8.4DT	+	+	■	■	■	0	■	0	■	-	-	■	0	0	■	+	■	■	■	■
9	+	0	+	+	0	+	+	+	■	+	0	+	+	0	+	0	+	+	0	+
10.1	0	0	■	+	+	+	+	+	■	0	0	+	0	+	+	0	+	+	0	+
10.2	-	0	■	+	0	+	+	+	■	0	+	+	0	+	+	0	+	+	+	+
10.3	+	0	■	0	0	+	+	+	■	0	0	+	0	+	+	0	+	+	0	+
10.4	0	-	■	0	-	+	■	0	■	0	0	0	+	+	+	+	+	+	0	+
11.1	+	0	+	+	+	+	+	+	+	■	0	+	+	+	+	+	+	+	-	+
11.2	(+)	+	(+)	+	+	+	+	+	+	■	+	+	+	+	+	+	+	+	0	+
11.3	+	0	+	+	+	+	+	+	+	(+)	(+)	+	+	+	+	+	+	+	0	+
12.1	+	+	+	+	+	+	+	+	+	+	+	+	(+)	+	+	+	+	+	(+)	+
12.2	+	+	+	+	+	+	+	(+)	+	■	0	+	■	+	+	+	+	+	(+)	■
12.3	(+)	0	+	+	0	(+)	0	(+)	+	+	0	+	+	-	+	+	0	0	0	■
12.4	-	0	(+)	-	-	-	0	0	0	0	0	0	■	0	0	+	0	0	-	■
13.1	(+)	(+)	■	-	(+)	-	-	-	0	-	-	-	-	-	0	-	-	+	-	-
13.2	+	+	■	0	+	+	(+)	0	+	+	0	+	0	+	+	+	0	+	0	(+)
13.3	+	+	■	(+)	+	+	-	0	(+)	(+)	0	+	0	+	0	+	+	+	0	(+)

	AU	BE	CY	DE	FI	FR	GE	GR	IC	IRL	IT	LU	MA	NL	NO	PO	SP	SW	TU	UK
13.4	0	+	■	(+)	+	+	0	0	0	0	0	0	-	-	0	-	-	+	0	-
14.1	+	(+)	+	0	+	(+)	+	+	0	(+)	(+)	(+)	+	+	+	+	+	+	0	+
14.2	+	(+)	+	+	+	+	+	+	0	+	(+)	+	+	+	+	+	+	+	+	+
15.1	+	-	+	0	0	+	+	0	+	0	+	0	+	+	+	0	0	+	■	+
15.2	+	-	+	+	0	+	+	0	0	+	0	0	+	+	+	0	0	+	■	+
16	-	0	■	-	-	0	-	0	0	0	-	0	-	0	0	0	0	+	-	0
17	+	(+)	■	+	+	-	-	+	+	(+)	+	0	-	+	+	+	+	+	0	+
18.1	(+)	0	■	+	+	+	+	+	+	+	+	0	■	+	■	+	(+)	+	0	+
18.2	+	(+)	■	+	+	+	-	-	0	0	+	0	■	+	■	+	0	+	-	+
18.3	■	0	■	-	(+)	+	+	-	0	-	+	0	■	+	■	+	(+)	-	-	-
18.4	+	+	■	+	+	+	+	0	+	+	+	+	+	+	■	+	+	+	0	+
19.1	+	(+)	+	■	+	+	+	+	■	+	+	+	■	+	+	+	+	+	0	+
19.2	+	0	(+)	■	(+)	+	(+)	+	■	+	+	0	■	+	+	+	+	+	0	+
19.3	+	0	(+)	■	+	(+)	+	+	■	+	+	+	■	+	-	+	+	+	0	+
19.4	■	0	+	■	0	+	-	0	■	+	-	+	■	+	0	-	0	+	-	-
19.5	+	+	+	■	+	+	+	+	■	+	-	+	■	+	+	+	+	+	0	+
19.6	-	-	(+)	■	(+)	0	-	-	■	-	-	0	■	0	0	0	0	0	0	-
19.7	■	+	(+)	■	+	+	(+)	+	■	+	+	-	■	+	+	-	+	+	0	+

	AU	BE	CY	DE	FI	FR	GE	GR	IC	IRL	IT	LU	MA	NL	NO	PO	SP	SW	TU	UK
19.8		+	(+)		+	+	0	0		-	+	0		+		+	0	-	-	-
19.9	+	+	+		+	+	+	+		+	+	+		+	+	+	+	+	(+)	+
19.10		-	(+)			0	-	-		-	-	-		0	-	-	0	-	-	-
PA 1				(1)*	0			(1)			0			0	0		(1)	0		
PA 2				(1)*	+			(1)			0			+	0		(1)	0		
PA 3				(1)*	+			(1)			0			+	0		(1)	+		
PA 4				(1)*	0			(1)			0				0		(1)	0		

65

The collective complaints procedure

The Additional Protocol to the European Social Charter providing for a system of collective complaints was opened for signature on 9 November 1995. It came into force on 1 July 1998. To date, seven states have ratified it: Cyprus, Finland, Greece, Italy, Norway, Portugal and Sweden. Slovenia has accepted to be bound by the procedure in application of Article D para. 2 of the revised Charter.

The purpose of the Protocol is to improve the efficiency of the supervisory machinery of the Social Charter by enabling collective complaints alleging violations of the Charter to be dealt with in addition to the current procedure for examining governments' reports.

1. **Collective complaints may be made by:**

   – international organisations of employers and trade unions which participate in the work of the Governmental Committee in pursuance of Article 27 para. 2 of the Charter ie. the European Trade Union Confederation (ETUC), the Union of Confederation of Industry and Employers of Europe (UNICE) and the International Organisation of Employers (IOE);

   – international non-governmental organisations with consultative status with the Council of Europe and appearing on a list drawn up for this purpose by the Governmental Committee;[1]

   – national organisations of employers and trade unions from the state concerned.

In addition, each state may, in a declaration to the Secretary General of the Council of Europe, authorise national non-governmental organisations to lodge complaints against it. To date, Finland has made such a declaration.

---

1. See Fact Sheet A – 14.

2. Form

There is no standard form for lodging collective complaints. They are lodged in writing and must be signed by an authorised representative of the complainant organisation.

3. Languages

The official languages of the Council of Europe are English and French.

Complaints lodged by the international employers' and trade union organisations participating in the work of the Governmental Committee (the European Trade Union Confederation (ETUC), the Union of Industrial and Employers' Confederations of Europe (UNICE) and the International Organisation of Employers (IOE)) or by international NGOs included in a list established for this purpose by the Governmental Committee must be written in English or French.

Complaints lodged by national employers' or trade union organisations or by national NGOs from the Contracting Party concerned may be submitted in a non-official language.

4. Content

Complaints must contain the following information:

- the name and contact details of the organisation lodging the complaint;
- in the case of NGOs, a mention that the organisation has consultative status with the Council of Europe and is included in the Governmental Committee list, and details of the fields in which it is active;
- the identity of the Contracting Party against which the complaint is being lodged (the state in question must have accepted the collective complaints procedure);
- a list of the Charter provisions concerned by the complaint (all of which must have been accepted by the state in question);
- the nature of the complaint (to what extent the state in question is alleged not to have ensured satisfactory application of certain Charter provisions);
- relevant arguments;
- copies of relevant documentation.

5. Procedure

Collective complaints are examined by the European Committee of Social Rights, Committee of Independent Experts of the Social Charter, which must first decide on their admissibility in the light of the criteria listed in the Protocol.

If the complaint is admissible the Committee examines the merits: after having collected information from the complainants, from the state concerned, from the other Contracting Parties to the Charter and from both sides of industry, draws up a report for the Committee of Ministers containing its conclusion as to whether or not the Contracting Party against which the complaint is directed has, in a satisfactory manner, ensured that the provision of the Charter which is the subject of the complaint is implemented.

It is then the task of the Committee of Ministers to adopt a resolution closing the procedure and, where appropriate, to address a recommendation to the Contracting Party concerned in the event that the European Committee of Social Rights finds that there has in fact been a breach of the Charter.

The Committee of Ministers may under specific circumstances consult the Governmental Committee (see Fact Sheet A – 8).

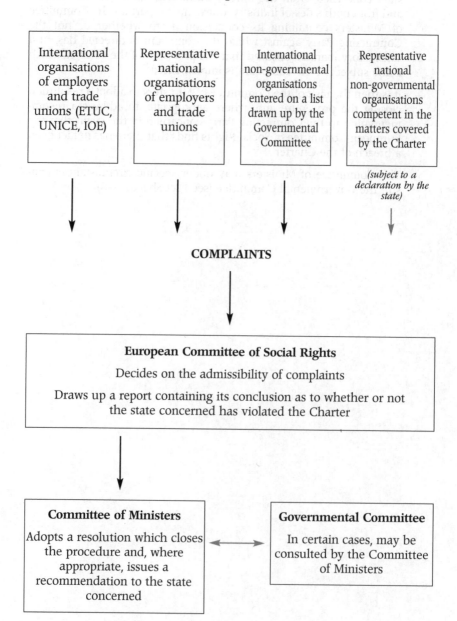

European Social Charter

Collective complaints procedure

International organisations of employers and trade unions (ETUC, UNICE, IOE)

Representative national organisations of employers and trade unions

International non-governmental organisations entered on a list drawn up by the Governmental Committee

Representative national non-governmental organisations competent in the matters covered by the Charter

(subject to a declaration by the state)

COMPLAINTS

European Committee of Social Rights

Decides on the admissibility of complaints

Draws up a report containing its conclusion as to whether or not the state concerned has violated the Charter

Committee of Ministers

Adopts a resolution which closes the procedure and, where appropriate, issues a recommendation to the state concerned

Governmental Committee

In certain cases, may be consulted by the Committee of Ministers

International non-governmental organisations entitled to submit collective complaints

1. List of NGOs entitled to submit collective complaints[1]

Conference of European Churches (KEK)

Eurolink Age

European Action of the Disabled (AEH) (1 January 2000)

European Antipoverty Network

European Association for Palliative Care (EAPC)

European Association of Railwaymen

European Centre of the International Council of Women

European Council of Police Trade Unions

European Council of WIZO Federations

European Federation of the Elderly (1 January 1999)

European Federation of Employees in Public Services (EUROFEDOP)

European Federation of National Organisations Working with the Homeless (FEANTSA)

European Forum for Child Welfare

Education International (1 January 1999)

European Movement

European Non-Governmental Sports Organisation (ENGSO) (1 January 1999)

European Ombudsman Institute

---

1. List established by the Governmental Committee following the decision of the Committee of Ministers on 22 June 1995 (see para. 20 of the explanatory report to the Protocol). The organisations are registered on this list – in English alphabetical order – for a duration of four years from the date of entry into force of the Protocol (1st July 1998), with the exception of five NGOs for which it is indicated that the duration of four years begins on 1st January 1999 or 1st January 2000.

European Organisation of Military Associations (EUROMIL)

European Regional Council of the World Federation for Mental Health

Eurotalent

European Union of Rechtspfleger (1 January 1999)

European Women's Lobby

International Association Autism-Europe

International Association of the Third-Age Universities

International Catholic Society for Girls

International Centre for the Legal Protection of Human Rights (INTERIGHTS)

International Commission of Jurists

International Confederation of Catholic Charities (CARITAS INTER-NATIONALIS) (1 January 2000)

International Council of Environmental Law (ICEL) (1 January 2000)

International Council of Nurses

International Council on Social Welfare

International Federation of Educative Communities (FICE)

International Federation of Human Rights Leagues

International Federation for Hydrocephalus and Spina Bifida

International Federation of Musicians

International Federation for Parent Education (1 January 1999)

International Federation of Settlements and Neighbourhood Centres

International Humanist and Ethical Union

International Movement ATD – Fourth World

International Planned Parenthood Federation – Europe Region (IPPF)

International Road Safety

International Scientific Conference of Minorities for Europe of Tomorrow (ISCOMET)

Marangopoulos Foundation for Human Rights (MFHR) (1 January 2000)

Public Services International

Quaker Council for European Affairs (QCEA)

Standing Committee of the Hospitals of the European Union

World Confederation of Teachers

2. Activities[1]

Conference of European Churches (KEK)

The Conference of European Churches is a regional ecumenical organisation of Anglican, Baptist, Lutheran, Methodist, Orthodox,

---

1. The brief description of activities was drafted by the Secretariat on the basis of information submitted by the NGOs with their applications.

Reformed, Catholic and Pentecostal churches. Its aim is to represent the views of churches on a wide variety of social issues, such as human rights, freedom of worship, European integration, economics, environment, etc.

Eurolink Age

Eurolink Age is a European network devoted to promoting and defending the rights and interests of the elderly.

European Action of the Disabled (AEH)

European Action of the Disabled groups together a score of European organisations working to promote equal rights and opportunities for people with disabilities and to improve the living conditions of the disabled and their families.

European Antipoverty Network

The aim of the European Antipoverty Network is to promote and develop concerted policies and action to combat all forms of poverty and social exclusion.

European Association for Palliative Care (EAPC)

The European Association for Palliative Care promotes the disciplines used in taking care of terminally ill patients, providing them with support at the end of their lives and assisting their families.

European Association of Railwaymen

The European Association of Railwaymen defends the social and economic rights of railwaymen in order to improve and harmonise their working conditions.

European Centre of the International Council of Women

The European Centre of the International Council of Women groups together national women's councils working to promote equality of rights and opportunities for women in society.

European Council of Police Trade Unions

The European Council of Police Trade Unions defends the rights and freedoms of policemen and -women, including freedom to join trade unions.

European Council of WIZO Federations

This international organisation of Zionist women's groups is made up of European organisations working to promote equality of rights and opportunities between women and men and to combat racism, xenophobia and anti-Semitism.

European Federation of the Elderly

The European Federation of the elderly defends the rights and interests of elderly people.

European Federation of Employees in Public Services (EUROFEDOP)

The European Federation of Employees in Public Services brings together national trade union organisations, representing and defending the rights and interests of public service staff.

European Federation of National Organisations Working with the Homeless (FEANTSA)

The European Federation of National Organisations Working with the Homeless is made up of national and regional associations working together to tackle the causes and eradicate the problem of homelessness in Europe.

European Forum for Child Welfare

The European Forum for Child Welfare brings together NGOs engaged in promoting and defending children's rights.

Education International

Education International is an association of national organisations which represents and defends the rights and interests of teachers.

European Movement

The European Movement is a group of national councils and associated European organisations whose common goal is to forge the democratic United States of Europe.

European Non-Governmental Sports Organisation (ENGSO)

The European Non-Governmental Sports Organisation groups together national sports confederations and Olympic committees whose aim, through a European policy on sport, is to promote democratic principles and social cohesion.

European Ombudsman Institute

The European Ombudsman Institute is an association of European Ombudsmen working together on issues related to human rights, the protection of citizens and the role of the Ombudsman.

European Organisation of Military Associations (EUROMIL)

The European Organisation of Military Associations brings together military associations in Europe concerned with promoting and defending the fundamental rights and freedoms of members of the armed forces, including freedom of association.

European Regional Council of the World Federation for Mental Health

The European Regional Council of the World Federation for Mental Health groups together European organisations whose purpose is to defend the rights of people suffering from mental disorder.

Eurotalent

Eurotalent is a group of European associations working to promote awareness of and provision for the specific problems and needs of exceptionally gifted children and adults.

European Union of Rechtspfleger

The European Union of Rechtspfleger groups together professional organisations of court officials with judicial or administrative functions. The union represents and defends the rights and interests of its members.

European Women's Lobby

The European Women's Lobby is an association of NGOs working to achieve effective equality of rights and opportunities between women and men.

International Association Autism-Europe

The International Association Autism-Europe is made up of associations of parents of autistic children. Its purpose is to defend the rights and interests of autistic people.

International Association of Third-Age Universities

The International Association of Third-Age Universities is an association of universities devoted to the promotion and development of the social integration of elderly people through a vast network of cultural and social exchange and information networks.

International Catholic Society for Girls

The International Catholic Society for Girls provides advice and assistance to young women to help them find their place and make their way in life and in society.

International Centre for the Legal Protection of Human Rights (INTERIGHTS)

"INTERIGHTS" is devoted to protecting human rights and fundamental freedoms, for example by helping victims to prepare and defend their cases before the national and international courts.

International Commission of Jurists

The International Commission of Jurists is a human rights organisation devoted to the promotion and protection of human rights and fundamental freedoms.

International Confederation of Catholic Charities (CARITAS INTERNATIONALIS)

"CARITAS" is a Catholic charity association which combats all forms of poverty and social exclusion and contributes to the promotion of social and economic rights and better living conditions for the very poor.

International Council of Environmental Law (ICEL)

The International Council of Environmental Law is a centre for information exchange between people and organisations concerned with the legal, administrative and political aspects of environmental protection.

International Council of Nurses

The International Council of Nurses groups together national associations of nurses with a view to defending the rights and interests of members of the nursing profession.

International Council on Social Welfare

The International Council on Social Welfare groups together national committees and international organisations concerned with promoting the economic and social rights of the most vulnerable members of society.

International Federation of Educative Communities

The International Federation of Educative Communities strives to defend children's rights and promote all forms of educational support to children and families.

International Federation of Human Rights Leagues

The International Federation of Human Rights Leagues is an organisation devoted to the promotion of human rights and fundamental freedoms.

International Federation for Hydrocephalus and Spina Bifida

The International Federation for Hydrocephalus and Spina Bifida groups together national associations working to improve the living conditions of persons suffering from this condition.

International Federation of Musicians

The International Federation of Musicians is a federation of European musicians' trade unions which defends the rights and interests of its members, particularly freedom to join trade unions and fair working conditions.

International Federation for Parent Education

The International Federation for Parent Education is a grouping of national associations to develop studies and research on family education with a view to informing and assisting parents in their educational role.

International Federation of Settlements and Neighbourhood Centres

The International Federation of Settlements and Neighbourhood Centres aims to eliminate social discrimination, promote equality of opportunity between people of different ethnic origins, develop public education and assist people in difficulty.

International Humanist and Ethical Union

Through its national and regional federations, the International Humanist and Ethical Union defends the principles and rights enshrined in the Universal Declaration of Human Rights, in particular the right to freedom of thought.

International Movement ATD – Fourth World

The International Movement ATD – Fourth World represents and defends the rights and interests of underprivileged families and combats poverty and social exclusion.

International Planned Parenthood Federation – Europe Region (IPPF)

The International Planned Parenthood Federation groups together associations whose aim is to promote and defend the right of all human beings to freedom of choice in matters of sexuality and reproduction.

International Road Safety

International Road Safety strives to promote co-operation between national road safety institutions and foster road accident prevention, for example through education, information and research.

International Scientific Conference of Minorities for Europe of Tomorrow (ISCOMET)

The International Scientific Conference of Minorities for Europe of Tomorrow brings together national associations whose aim is to promote and defend the rights and interests of minorities and ethnic groups.

Marangopoulos Foundation for Human Rights (MFHR)

The Marangopoulos Foundation for Human Rights is a European foundation devoted to the defence, promotion and protection of human rights and fundamental freedoms.

Public Services International

Public Services International is a federation of public service trade unions from about a hundred countries. Its role is to defend the rights and interests of its members.

Quaker Council for European Affairs (QCEA)

The Quaker Council for European Affairs is an international association of a religious, educational and philanthropic nature, devoted to promoting the values of the Religious Society of Friends in the European context.

Standing Committee of the Hospitals of the European Union

The Standing Committee of the Hospitals of the European Union groups together national hospital associations and representatives of national or regional health authorities devoted to promoting public health.

World Confederation of Teachers

The World Confederation of teachers groups together teachers' trade unions which represent and defend the rights and interests of their members.

Part B
States' implementation of the Charter

Signature of the European Social Charter or of the revised Social Charter

1. The choice of instrument

In its opinions on states' requests for membership of the Organisation over the past several years, the Parliamentary Assembly of the Council of Europe has invited states to study the Social Charter with a view to preparing for its ratification and in this context to implement policies which are in conformity with the principles enshrined in the treaty. When Lithuania and Andorra became members in 1993 and 1994 respectively, the Parliamentary Assembly indicated that it expected the authorities of both countries to sign and ratify the Charter rapidly. More recently, the Parliamentary Assembly gave a precise deadline for the procedure. Thus in April 1999 Georgia became the forty-first member state of the Council of Europe and has undertaken to sign and ratify the Charter within a time limit of three years. In addition, the campaign launched by the Assembly in May 1997 to obtain the largest possible number of ratifications of the Charter and the revised Charter by member states achieved positive results.

Thirty-seven of the forty-one states in the Organisation have now either signed or ratified the Charter or the revised Charter; the other states have announced their intention of doing so in the very near future.

The new member states have the choice of which instrument to ratify: the 1961 Social Charter or the revised Charter of 1996?

Several of the new states have already responded: thus on 26 June 1997 Poland was the first state from central and eastern Europe to ratify the 1961 Charter, followed on 22 June 1998 by Slovakia, 8 July 1999 by Hungary and 3 November 1999 by the Czech Republic.

Other states have preferred to immediately turn to the 1996 revised Charter, as have Bulgaria, Romania and Slovenia. Albania, Estonia, Lithuania, Moldova and Ukraine have also opted for the revised

Charter which they have signed and which they are preparing to ratify.

2. Why the 1996 revised Charter?

The national authorities have the choice of the instrument, and they must also decide in the light of legislation and practice the provisions they wish to accept.

Until the entry into force of the revised Charter on 1st July 1999, it appeared too early for new member states to select a text that did not yet have the required number of ratifications to enter into force. This issue is no longer relevant and should prompt states to prefer the revised Charter.

The revised Charter is the only treaty to guarantee all aspects of fundamental social and economic rights. Taking into account the changes which have come about over the past thirty years in the field of social rights, this modern instrument has remedied the lacunae of the 1961 Charter and is presently a European instrument for the protection of human rights fully adapted to the realities of the 21st century.

Furthermore, the treaty combines in a single instrument all the rights guaranteed in the Charter of 1961 and the Additional Protocol of 1988, as well as amendments to these rights and new rights. It also allows states to declare themselves bound by the Additional Protocol providing for a system of collective complaints by notification. The ratification procedure before national parliaments is thus considerably simplified.

The 1996 revised Charter is intended to replace in time the 1961 Charter, although they will co-exist for a certain period. It therefore seems appropriate that new member states directly proceed towards signature and ratification of the revised Charter.

3. How do states sign the Charter?

As in the case of all the treaties within the Council of Europe, the Social Charter, its Protocols and the revised Charter may be signed by:

- the Prime Minister or the Minister of Foreign Affairs of the state concerned,
- a minister or ambassador of the state concerned empowered to do so and who has been invested with full authority by the Minister of Foreign Affairs.

Signature may take place at any time, in the presence of the Secretary General of the Council of Europe or of his or her representative.

When the decision to sign has been taken and the internal formalities completed, the state concerned must make an appointment with the Secretary General by the intermediary of the Treaty Office of the Directorate General I – Legal Affairs.

At the time of signature it is not compulsory to communicate the provisions which the state intends to accept upon ratification.

It should be pointed out that signature is above all a political gesture showing a state's intention of examining the treaty in view of ratification and of submitting the text to Parliament to this end.

In international law, signature does not oblige a state to implement the treaty, but does mean that it should demonstrate its "good faith" in relation to it. Signatory states are also entitled, in the same way as states having ratified it, to raise objections against reservations made by states ratifying the Charter or the revised Charter. Such objections are possible on condition that the signatory state considers a reservation counter to the objectives or the aim of the treaty.

4. The consequences of signature

Any state which signs the Charter or the revised Charter is invited to attend meetings of the Governmental Committee of the Social Charter as an observer (see Fact Sheet A – 8).

Selection of articles

1. Obligation to accept a minimum number of provisions

One of the first tasks of states when beginning the process of ratification of the Charter consists in determining whether they are in a position to accept all the provisions of the treaty or whether a selection of provisions should be made.

Taking into account the differences between social and economic structures in the European states, the Charter does not insist on the immediate acceptation of all the Articles. A flexible system allows states to make a choice between them, whilst obliging them to accept a hard core of undertakings considered to be the most fundamental: they may in this way extend their commitments progressively at a later date.

The minimum number of provisions to be accepted differs according to the chosen instrument.

Under Article 20 of the 1961 Charter, states must accept at least five of the seven following Articles: Articles 1, 5, 6, 12, 13, 16 and 19 (these Articles are known as the "hard core") and a number of supplementary Articles or numbered paragraphs. The total number of Articles or numbered paragraphs may not be less than ten Articles or forty-five numbered paragraphs.

Article A of the revised Charter – which corresponds to Article 20 of the 1961 Charter – has added Articles 7 and 20 to the "hard core". The "hard core" of the revised Charter thus consists of Articles 1, 5, 6, 7, 12, 13, 16, 19 and 20, from which states must accept at least six Articles: in addition, states must accept a further number of provisions to bring the total accepted to at least sixteen Articles or sixty-three numbered paragraphs.

Two approaches to acceptance are possible:

– a limited number of provisions may be accepted, for instance the minimum required by the 1961 Charter or the revised Charter. In this case, a state will choose the provisions which do not represent difficulties. It is hoped that the state will go on to accept further Articles or paragraphs as legislative, social and economic progress takes place. Further provisions can be accepted at any time by notifying the Secretary General of the Council of Europe;

– all the Charter or revised Charter provisions may be immediately accepted. As the Charter is an instrument for the defence of human rights, every state should endeavour to attain the highest level of undertakings required. The two-year interval between ratification and the submission of the first report on the application of the Charter may be usefully employed in filling gaps which remain in national law and practices.

Six states have so far accepted all the provisions of the Charter either upon ratification or by accepting supplementary provisions at a later date: Belgium, France, Italy, Portugal, the Netherlands and Spain.

For the moment, France is the only country to have accepted all the provisions of the revised Charter.

2. How are the provisions selected?

The first stage consists in examining the provisions of the Charter and comparing them with national legislation and practice, and with the relevant case law. Compatibility studies are usually carried out by the public servants responsible for the ratification process. Inter-ministerial committees composed of representatives of different ministries, social partners, NGOs and experts are set up for the purpose.

It is important to involve all the persons concerned in the preparatory phase and in particular the representatives of employers and trade unions and the main national NGOs, who will play a role in the follow-up to supervision of the Charter commitments.

During the second stage, a more in-depth examination is conducted aimed to clarify certain points of case law, sometimes with the help of the Council of Europe. At the request of the national authorities, a team of experts on the Charter is set up to assess the conformity of national legislation and practice with the Charter, and to present in detail the case law of the European Committee of Social Rights. Since 1996 seminars of this kind have been held in most of the new member states.

Compatibility studies may take several forms: workshops concentrating on certain provisions of the Charter, workshops on specific aspects of the legislation and practice of the state concerned or on issues with particular importance for the state. Legislative assessments may be made of laws or bills on matters related to the Charter and to decide which propositions to adopt in order to bring existing norms into line. In this way the ratification procedure can contribute to accelerating the reform processes under way.

On completion of these studies, the competent authorities are ready to decide which Articles will be accepted on ratification.

Ratification of the European Social Charter and of the revised Social Charter

The European Social Charter enters into force in a state when the government ratifies it by depositing an instrument of ratification. The ratification procedure in each state depends on its constitutional law. A bill on ratification is normally presented to parliament after approval by the government.

Following enactment of the bill on ratification, the state prepares an instrument of ratification.

The instrument of ratification must specify which provisions the state has accepted and in which of its territories the treaty will apply. This information may also be given in a letter accompanying the instrument of ratification. Other declarations or reservations may also be attached (see Fact Sheet B – 4).

The instrument of ratification is deposited with the Secretary General of the Council of Europe.

1. Procedure for depositing an instrument of ratification

To deposit its instrument of ratification, the state must make an appointment with the Secretary General through the Treaty Office of the Directorate General I – Legal Affairs. Any person so authorised by the state concerned may deposit the instrument.

It is usually the Permanent Representative to the Council of Europe who does this, but it may be a minister or sometimes the Prime Minister.

The ratification ceremony may take place at any time. In order to invest it with a certain solemnity, it may be planned to coincide with the twice-yearly meeting of the Ministers of Foreign Affairs, or with a session of the Parliamentary Assembly of the Council of Europe.

2. Entry into force

The Charter and the revised Charter contain provisions concerning their entry into force in respect of a new Contracting Party:

- under Article 35 of the Charter, the treaty comes into force as from the thirtieth day after the date of deposit of its instrument of ratification or approval;

- Article K of the revised Charter provides for it to enter into force on the first day of the month following expiry of a period of one month after the date of deposit of the instrument of ratification, acceptance or approval.

Declarations and reservations

1. Definition of a declaration

A declaration is an act whereby a state, when ratifying, accepting or approving the Charter or the revised Charter or at any time thereafter, specifies the scope of the obligations it accepts.

2. Compulsory declaration upon ratification

The state must declare which provisions of the Charter or revised Charter it accepts.

This declaration must be made at the time of ratification. It may be made at the time of signature, but this is not an obligation.

3. Optional declarations

A. Territorial application

States may extend the application of the Charter or revised Charter, by declaration, to certain non-metropolitan parts of their territory.

B. Extension of the personal scope

States may declare that the Charter or revised Charter also applies to persons other than those covered by the Appendix (for example to all persons within their jurisdiction).

C. Protocol providing for a system of collective complaints: national NGOs

States may declare that representative national non-governmental organisations within their jurisdiction have the right to lodge collective complaints against them.

D. Revised Charter: collective complaints

States which are not bound by the Protocol providing for a system of collective complaints may, when depositing their instruments of ratification, acceptation or approval of the revised Charter or at any other time thereafter, declare that they accept the supervision of their obligations under the revised Charter according to the procedure provided for in the said Protocol.

E. *Acceptance of new provisions*

States may declare at any time that they accept additional articles or numbered paragraphs.

4. Definition of a reservation

A reservation is a declaration whereby a state, when ratifying, accepting or approving the Charter or revised Charter, precludes or modifies the legal effect of certain provisions of the treaty as applied within its territory.

Reservations may be made only on the occasion of the deposit of the instrument of ratification.

Furthermore, a state may not enter reservations when accepting the minimum number of provisions for conformity with Article 20 of the Charter or Article A of the revised Charter. Reservations may thus be made by a state only in respect of additional provisions it accepts.

For the full texts of the declarations and reservations made by the states which have ratified the Charter, its Protocols and the revised Charter, see the Collected Texts, published by the Council of Europe (new edition) and the Charter's web site: http://www.socialcharter.coe.int.

Ratification of the revised Charter by states having previously ratified the Charter and/or Protocol No. 1

1. Obligation to accept at least the same provisions

In order to ensure that, when ratifying the revised Charter, states do not implicitly denounce certain articles or paragraphs of the Charter and/or Protocol No. 1 which they had previously accepted, Article B of Part III of the revised Charter requires them to accept at least the provisions which correspond to those of the Charter and/or Protocol No. 1 by which they were previously bound.

However, it is always possible for states, before ratifying the revised Charter, to denounce certain provisions of the Charter and/or Protocol No. 1, but they must do so explicitly and follow the procedure laid down in Articles 37 of the Charter and 11 of Protocol No. 1.

2. Correspondence between provisions

The provisions of the revised Charter correspond to those with the same Article or paragraph number in the Charter, except for the following:

- Article 3 para. 2 of the revised Charter corresponds to Article 3 paras. 1 and 3 of the Charter;

- Article 3 para. 3 of the revised Charter corresponds to Article 3 paras. 2 and 3 of the Charter;

- Article 10 para. 5 of the revised Charter corresponds to Article 10 para. 4 of the Charter;

- Article 17 para. 1 of the revised Charter corresponds to Article 17 of the Charter.

Articles 20 to 23 of the revised Charter correspond to the provisions of Articles 1 to 4 of Protocol No. 1.

3. Transition from one reporting system to the other

When a state bound by the Charter ratifies the revised Charter, the last report it must submit on the Charter concerns the reference period prior to the date of entry into force of the revised Charter for that state (see Fact Sheet B – 7 (1)).

Thereafter, it submits reports on the application of the revised Charter (see Fact Sheet B – 7 (2)).

Follow-up to ratification

Ratification of the Charter entails several obligations. The main requirements are to take the necessary steps to ensure the application of the accepted provisions, to prepare the first report on the Charter's implementation and to take part in meetings of the Governmental Committee.

1. Application of the Charter

During preparations for ratification, a complete inventory of current legislation and practice will have been drawn up. Between the Charter's entry into force and submission of the initial report on its application, the possibility remains of eliminating any discrepancies that might exist between Charter obligations and the state of law and practice, and of introducing appropriate measures that will give full force to accepted provisions.

In addition, supervisory mechanisms must be set up in respect of obligations and in particular the services of the Labour Inspectorate must carry out their duties properly and be provided where necessary with adequate financial and human resources.

A number of authorities (ministries, the Labour Inspectorate, the courts and government offices) must be informed that the Charter has entered into force, and the departments concerned must be given appropriate instructions relating to administrative procedure (for example, ensuring that nationals of all the other Contracting Party effectively receive equal treatment).

2. Drafting reports

The main responsibility is then to prepare the first report and subsequent periodical reports.

Many different ministries and institutions are involved in the preparation of reports – the Ministries of Labour, Social Affairs, Health and

Education, Justice, Labour Inspectorate, local and regional authorities, etc. – which means that co-ordination is an important feature.

The role of the co-ordinator or the co-ordination unit is to gather all information necessary for drafting the report, to ensure consultation with representative employers' and labour organisations and that deadlines are respected. It is vital that reports be submitted on time and in one of the official languages of the Council of Europe (English or French).

At a later stage, the co-ordination unit will forward the Conclusions of the European Committee of Social Rights to the appropriate government offices as soon as they are received, drawing attention to the general and specific questions to be answered in the next report. It will also collate all information the representative to the Governmental Committee will need.

3. Meetings of the Governmental Committee

As soon as the Charter or the revised Charter has been signed, states are invited to appoint a representative to attend Governmental Committee meetings as an observer.[1]

The Governmental Committee meets three or four times every year. The meetings usually last four or five days and are held in the Human Rights Building in Strasbourg in accordance with a calendar agreed by the Governmental Committee. Observers play an active role in meetings, being free to speak and express their viewpoint, but they have no voting rights.

Once the Charter or the revised Charter has been ratified, government representatives can participate fully in the Charter's supervisory machinery and are required to give an opinion, sometimes by voting, on all the issues and national situations as and when they come before the Governmental Committee. It is the task of the representative of the country under examination to provide the Governmental Committee with all useful information which will allow it to decide, on the basis of social, economic and other policy considerations, how the conclusions of the European Committee of Social Rights should be followed up (see Fact Sheets A – 8 and B – 9).

---

1. There may be several representatives from each state on the Committee, but the Council of Europe covers the travel and subsistence expenses of one expert per country only (for states having ratified the Charter or the revised Charter and the states of central and eastern Europe who have signed either instrument).

The system for the submission of reports

1. Social Charter

A. *General remarks*

According to Article 21 of the Social Charter, Contracting Parties are required to send a report to the Secretary General of the Council of Europe every second year concerning the implementation of the provisions of the Charter they have accepted. A Form for Reports adopted by the Committee of Ministers serves as the framework for supplying the information required in assessing states' compliance with the Charter. The supervisory system functioned on this basis for the first eight supervision cycles (1965-1981).

B. *Background*

The steady increase in the number of Contracting Parties started to cause delays in the functioning of the supervisory mechanism. A solution was adopted in 1984 by the Committee of Ministers, whereby states were divided into two groups, submitting their reports in alternate years. For this reason, the Conclusions for the ninth to twelfth supervision cycles were published in two parts, each of them concerning one of the two groups of states.

In 1992 further action was needed in view of the even greater number of Contracting Parties. The Committee of Ministers consequently decided to introduce a new system of reporting for a trial period of four years, under which Contracting Parties were required to submit a report every year on a selection of provisions. However, all the Contracting Parties did not accept this system: it was decided that Germany would submit a full report every two years.

The new Contracting Parties were asked to submit two full reports before joining the system of partial reports.

C. Current system

By the end of the trial period, a new system for the presentation of reports was agreed unanimously by the Contracting Parties to the Charter. Under this system, all Contracting Parties report on the same provisions at the same time. The advantage of this system is that it allows a comparison to be made between the different national situations with respect to each Charter provision.

After ratification, a new Contracting Party to the Charter must submit a first report covering all the provisions of the Charter. A second full report is to be submitted two years after the first report. The states will subsequently follow the normal cycle for submission of reports, ie. a report every two years on the hard core provisions and a report every four years on the provisions outside the hard core.

As shown in the tables below, Contracting Parties may submit a report every year or combine their reports on the hard core and on the other provisions for presentation every second year. This system entered into force in June 1997.

Supervision cycle XV

States concerned	Articles	Reference period	Submission of reports	Publication of Conclusions	Publication of Governemental Committee reports	Decisions of the Committee of Ministers
All Contracting Parties XV-1	1. Hard core: Articles 1, 5, 6, 12, 13, 16 and 19 (except Article 1 par. 4)	1997 – 1998[1]	30 June 1999	28 February 2000	October 2000	December 2000
All Contracting Parties XV-2	2. Half of non-hard core: Articles 7, 8, 11, 14, 17 and 18 + Articles 1 and 4 of Additional Protocol	1995 – 1998[1]	either 30 June 1999 or 31 March 2000	31 December 2000	October 2001	December 2001

1. The begining of the reference period depends on the reference period of the last report on the provision concerned.

Supervision cycle XVI

States concerned	Articles	Reference period	Submission of reports	Publication of Conclusions	Publication of Governemental Committee reports	Decisions of the Committee of Ministers
All Contracting Parties XVI-1	1. Hard core	1999 – 2000	30 June 2001	28 February 2002	October 2002	December 2002
All Contracting Parties XVI-2	2. Half of non-hard core: Articles 2, 3, 4, 9, 10 and 15 + Articles 2 and 3 of Additional Protocol	1997 – 2000	either 30 June 2001 or 31 March 2002	31 December 2002	October 2003	December 2003

System for the presentation of reports on the application of the European Social Charter from cycle XV-1

Supervision cycles	Date of submission of reports	First 20 Contracting Parties	Poland	Slovakia	Hungary, Czech Republic	States ratifying between 1/4/2000 and 30/6/2001
XV-1	30 June 1999	Hard core	1st report (full)			
XV-2	31 March 2000	1st part of other provisions[1]		31/7/2000 1st report (full)		
XVI-1	30 June 2001	Hard core[2]	2nd report (full)			
XVI-2	31 March 2002	2nd part of other provisions[3]	3rd report (2nd part of other provisions)	31/7/2000 2nd report (full)	1st report (full)	
XVII-1	30 June 2003	Hard core[4]	4th report (hard core)	3rd report (hard core)		1st report (full)
XVII-2	31 March 2004	1st part of other provisions[5]	5th report (1st part of other provisions)	4th report (1st part of other provisions)	2nd report (full)	
XVIII-1	30 June 2005	Hard core	6th report (hard core)	5th report (hard core)	3rd report (hard core)	2nd report (full)
XVIII-2	31 March 2006	2nd part of other provisions	7th report (2nd part of other provisions)	6th report (2nd part of other provisions)	4th report (2nd part of other provisions)	3rd report (2nd part of other provisions)

1. Last report on the 1961 Social Charter of Sweden, Italy and France.
2 The first 20 Contracting Parties to the Charter except Sweden, Italy and France (1st reports on the hard core of the revised Social Charter).
3 Last report on the 1961 Social Charter for states who ratified the revised Social Charter between 1/7/1999 and 31/3/2000.
4 Last report on the 1961 Social Charter for states who ratify the revised Social Charter between 1/4/2000 and 30/6/2001.
5 Last report on the 1961 Social Charter for states who ratify the revised Social Charter between 1/7/2000 and 31/3/2002.

2. Revised Social Charter

The Committee of Ministers has adopted a system for the presentation of reports on the revised Charter parallel to that of the Charter.

The system functions as follows:

– a report every two years on the hard core (30 June of odd years);
– a report every four years on the other provisions (31 March of even years, alternately with the other half of the provisions concerned).

The provisions of the hard core are Articles 1, 5, 6, 7, 12, 13, 16, 19 and 20.

The other provisions are divided into two groups:

– Articles 2, 3, 4, 9, 10, 15, 21, 22, 24, 26, 28, 29, ie. 12 Articles and 31 paragraphs;
– Articles 8, 11, 14, 17, 18, 23, 25, 27, 30, 31, ie. 10 Articles and 26 paragraphs.

The first reports will be submitted :

– by 30 June 2001 for the hard core;
– by 31 March 2002 for the first part of the other provisions;
– by 30 June 2003 for the hard core;
– by 31 March 2004 for the second half of the other provisions, etc.

In contrast to the situation with regard to the Social Charter, states who ratify the revised Charter are not obliged to submit two full reports before adopting the system of partial reports.

However, to avoid a too long period between entry into force and the date at which the European Committee of Social Rights has the opportunity to examine all the provisions accepted by a state, the first report on the non-hard core provisions exceptionally covers all of them. These reports are shown in bold in the table overleaf.

System for the presentation of reports on the application of the revised Social Charter: proposal made by the European Committee of Social Rights

System for the presentation of reports on the application of the revised Social Charter

Supervision cycle	Date of submission of reports	Provisions	Reference period[1]	France, Italy, Romania, Slovenia and Sweden	Bulgaria	Estonia, Cyprus and states ratifying before 30/6/2001	States ratifying between 1/7/2001 and 31/3/2002
1	30 June 2001	Hard core	1999-2000	1st report			
2	31 March 2002	First part of other provisions	1999-2000	**2nd report[2]**	**1st report[2]**		
3	30 June 2003	Hard core	2001-2002	3rd report	2nd report	1st report	
4	31 March 2004	Second part of other provisions	2001-2002	4th report	3rd report	**2nd report[2]**	**1st report[2]**
5	30 June 2005	Hard core	2003-2004	5th report	4th report	3rd report	2nd report
6	31 March 2006	First part of other provisions	2001-2004	6th report	5th report	4th report	4th report
7	30 June 2007	Hard core	2005-2006	7th report	6th report	5th report	4e rapport
8	31 March 2008	Second part of other provisions	2003-2006	8th report	7th report	6th report	5th report

1. To be adapted according to the date of entry into force of the revised Social Charter for each state.
2. The reports in bold indicate that the first report exceptionally covers all the non-hard core provisions.

National reports

After ratifying the Charter or the revised Charter, Contracting Parties must submit a first report to the Secretary General of the Council of Europe then, at regular intervals, further reports describing how national law and practice ensure the implementation of the accepted provisions.

Reports are requested in a letter sent by the Secretariat of the Council of Europe to the states' permanent representations to the Council of Europe. A copy of the letter is forwarded to the government representatives on the Governmental Committee. The letter lists the Articles and the reference period to be covered in the report, a reminder of any general questions asked by the European Committee of Social Rights during the preceding supervision cycle, and the deadline for submission.

Reports are drawn up along the lines of forms. There are three forms for the presentation of national reports: one for the 1961 Charter, which has recently been revised;[1] one for the Additional Protocol of 1988 and another for the revised Charter. See the *Collected Texts* (new edition) published by the Council of Europe for the text of the forms. Each report must contain information in reply to the questions on the Form for Reports and to all those asked by the European Committee of Social Rights. Any legislation, statistics and other relevant documents must be included in appendices.

Reports must be submitted in one of the two official languages of the Council of Europe (French or English). The same applies, as far as possible, to the appendices. Reports must be sent by e-mail to the following address: social.charter@coe.int in Word for PC format or on

---

1. The revised Form for Reports on the Social Charter will apply as from the XVI-1 cycle of supervision (reports submitted by 20 June 2001). This is also the date for the submission of first reports on the application of the revised Social Charter.

a diskette, or failing this five paper copies may be submitted (two of the appendices).

Statistical information compiled to other international organisations (ILO, OECD, EUROSTAT) may be included for information purposes. It may also be useful to attach copies of reports made for the ILO or the United Nations where they refer to provisions similar to those of the Charter.

Copies of the reports must be sent to the employers' and workers' organisations which are affiliated to the organisations holding observer status with the Governmental Committee (ETUC, UNICE and IOE). This must be done sufficiently early to permit these organisations to submit their comments within the deadline. It is permissible for such comments to be sent directly to the Secretary General of the Council of Europe, and the Charter Secretariat will then forward a copy to the government concerned so that it can reply. Copies of reports may also be sent to national NGOs.

As soon as a report is received by the Secretary General it becomes public. It is distributed to anyone who so requests and appears of the Internet site (http://socialcharter.coe.int).

Follow-up to conclusions

Once the European Committee of Social Rights adopts its conclusions these are transmitted to the Contracting Parties and made public. There are three types of conclusion – positive, negative and deferred. States should carefully study all conclusions that concern them. Similarly, states should read the general introduction to each volume of Conclusions to see whether any points or questions of general concern have been raised by the Committee.

1. Positive conclusion

A positive conclusion indicates adequate implementation of the Charter provision concerned. Nevertheless, the Committee often includes questions to governments or requests for information. Where this situation arises, the follow-up will consist of providing all the requested information and explanations in the subsequent report for that provision.

2. Deferred conclusion

A conclusion will be deferred when the Committee does not have the information required to make an assessment of compliance. The necessary elements must be supplied in the next report. Failure to do so could lead to a negative conclusion on the ground that the state has not demonstrated its compliance with the Charter. Repeated lack of information may lead the Governmental Committee to issue a warning or propose that a recommendation be issued by the Committee of Ministers to the state concerned.

3. Negative conclusion

A negative conclusion means that the situation in the state concerned is not in conformity with the Charter. The appropriate steps to remedy this situation will depend on the source and nature of the problem (legislation, administrative practice, case law, etc.). Since the Governmental Committee considers all negative conclusions in the months following publication, the state concerned should be in a position at that stage to describe the steps that will be taken to rectify the situation. The next national report on the provision concerned should also indicate the measures taken to bring the situation into conformity with the Charter. If these have not yet taken effect, the state should indicate the timetable for compliance

Follow-up to warnings

According to its working methods, the Governmental Committee may address warnings to states which fail to conform to the Charter or which fail to supply the information needed for the European Committee of Social Rights to assess the national situation's compliance with the Charter (see Fact Sheet A – 7).

1. **Warning in the event of a negative conclusion (non-conformity with the Charter)**

Each negative conclusion of the European Committee of Social Rights is examined by the Governmental Committee. Following discussion and in the light of the information supplied by the country's representative, the Governmental Committee usually takes a vote on whether or not it should suggest addressing a recommendation to the state concerned. If there is no majority in favour of a recommendation, the Governmental Committee may decide to issue a warning to the state.

When the national situation criticised concerns a Contracting Party whose report is the subject of the first conclusions of the European Committee of Social Rights on a particular provision, the Governmental Committee addresses a warning to the state rather than proposing a recommendation. This gives the state time to study the conclusions and take the necessary steps.

When a warning follows a negative conclusion, it is an indication that the state should take steps to discharge its obligations under the Charter, failing which a recommendation could be proposed on the occasion of the following supervision cycle.

2. **Warning in the event of a deferred conclusion (repeated lack of information)**

National situations in respect of which the European Committee of Social Rights has had to defer its conclusion several times for repeated lack of information are examined by the Governmental Committee, which may decide to issue a warning in order to prompt the country to provide all the relevant information in its next report. If the required information is still not forthcoming, a recommendation may be proposed on the occasion of the following supervision cycle.

Follow-up to recommendations

Where a situation, which was the subject of a negative conclusion, has not been remedied, the Committee of Ministers can decide, on a proposal from the Governmental Committee, to address a recommendation to the state concerned.

The recommendation requests that the state concerned take appropriate action to remedy the situation. The obligation is contained in the text of the recommendation itself, which requests that the state take account, in an appropriate manner, of the negative conclusion of the European Committee of Social Rights and provide information in its next report on the measures it has taken to this effect.

The European Committee of Social Rights supervises the follow-up given to recommendations by examining the steps taken to remedy the situation criticised.

In the case of a renewal of the negative conclusion, the Governmental Committee may repeat its proposal for a recommendation.

Recommendations are an effective means of guaranteeing compliance with the Charter. Firstly, they have a dissuasive effect, as states endeavour to find appropriate solutions to situations which have been criticised even before a recommendation is made, in order to avoid its adoption.

Examples of situations in which adoption of a recommendation by the Committee of Ministers has led to changes and plans for reform

- In Greece, work is under way on a bill to amend legislation providing for criminal sanctions against seafarers (Recommendations RChS (93) 1 and RChS (95) 4).
- In Austria, maternity legislation was amended by the supplementary Act on the right to work, which guarantees identical protection for domestic employees, whether or not they live in their employers' homes (Recommendation RChS (94) 1).

- In France, a reform of the Code of the Merchant Navy is in preparation (Recommendations RChS (94) 2 and RChs (95) 3).
- In Italy, a reform is in progress in the area of child labour to remedy the situation of children engaged in agriculture and domestic work (Recommendation RChS (94) 4).
- Again in Italy, a bill is being prepared to repeal the provisions of the Navigation Code (Recommendations RChS (94) 4 and RChS (95) 7). In addition, a bill on the establishment of a social assistance scheme is under examination (Recommendation RChS (94) 4).
- In Spain, the National Ports and Merchant Navy Act No. 27 of 24 November 1992 repealed the Penal and Disciplinary Act of 22 December 1955 on the merchant navy, which provided for criminal sanctions against seamen (Recommendation RChS (94) 5).
- In Greece, the 1989 Act on child labour is being reformed so as to cover children engaged in agricultural, forestry or livestock work of a family nature (Recommendation RChS (95) 5). In addition, Act No. 2446 of 20 October 1998 introduced a social insurance scheme (Recommendation RChS (93) 1 and RChS (95) 4).
- In Ireland, Act No. 20 (1998) on the merchant navy repealed the provisions of the 1894 Merchant Shipping Act, which provided for criminal sanctions against seamen (Recommendation RChS (95) 6).
- In Malta, changes are being made to the law in order to improve police officers' trade-union rights and adapt the machinery for voluntary negotiations (Recommendation RChS (97) 1).
- In the United Kingdom, the provisions of the Merchant Shipping Act enabling criminal sanctions to be imposed on seamen will soon be repealed (Recommendation RChS (97) 3).
- In Turkey, work is under way on a bill to amend the Civil Code (Recommendation RChS (98) 4).
- In France, a bill is being prepared to eliminate the differences that still remain between the inheritance rights of children born in and out of marriage (Recommendation RChS (98) 1).

The social partners

The text of the Charter (Article 23) lays down the obligation on states to communicate copies of their reports to social partner organisations which are members of the organisations invested with observer status on the Governmental Committee, namely ETUC, IOE and UNICE. Article 1 of the Amending Protocol of 1991 amends Article 23 para. 2 by allowing for the direct transmission of the social partners' comments to the Secretary General of the Council of Europe, rather than having to pass through the government. It is already implemented in practice.

The governments have the opportunity to reply to these comments.

There are several means for the social partners to be associated with the drafting of reports. For example, if there is a committee of officials responsible for preparing the report, social partner representatives could be invited to participate. Alternatively, a meeting could be held on national implementation of the Charter provisions under review prior to the final drafting of the report. Trade union and employer research or publications could be referred to in the report or appended to it, in an effort to reflect the perspective of both sides of industry.

Social partner involvement will be consolidated if they are associated with the follow-up to conclusions and with the procedures which aim to bring national situations into line with the Charter after a negative conclusion has been reached.

Non-governmental organisations

While social partner organisations are to be consulted on the basis of the text of the Charter itself, consultation of NGOs is not provided for. However, since the protection of civil and political human rights goes far beyond labour issues, NGOs can make an important contribution to national reports (for example, social welfare issues, family policy, the protection of children, health services, etc.). As with social partners, NGO publications could be quoted in national reports or appended to them, where appropriate.

Under the Amending Protocol of 1991, national reports are to be sent to the organisations which have consultative status in the Council of Europe. In fact, as reports are public documents, they are available to any organisation on request to the Secretariat of the Social Charter. They are also available on the Internet.

As a gesture of recognition of the opinions of civil society, states may inform NGOs in good time of the contents of the report and encourage them to make comments. Good practice along these lines would be in keeping with the vital role – recognised by the Council of Europe – of such organisations in defending human rights.

Non-governmental organizations

The ADACS programme

Since the transformation of Europe in 1989 and the accession of new member states, the Council of Europe has made efforts to consolidate democratic reform, which entails institutional, legislative and administrative review. This promotion has entailed the organisation of a wide range of activities, including expert meetings, workshops, training courses and study visits.

Initially, activities were organised to help the new member states to meet their statutory obligations on entry into the Council of Europe, and to provide applicant states with the necessary guidance and information to facilitate accession. To this end, an annual programme of activities was planned to attempt to meet the needs of these states.

Now that a great majority of applicant states have joined the Council of Europe, their needs have changed, becoming more akin to those of the other member states. In addition, the Second Summit of Heads of State and Government, held in Strasbourg on 10 and 11 October 1997, put particular focus on supporting the Council of Europe's contribution to cohesion, stability and security in Europe. In December 1997, in order to mirror these changes, the Committee of Ministers decided to give the name "Activities for the Development and Consolidation of Democratic Stability" (ADACS) to these activities, and to extend them to all the member states of the Council of Europe and to the applicant countries.

The ADACS programme comprises different subject areas, one of which is the human rights activities programme.

Specific activities on the European Social Charter have been organised since 1994. The annually increasing number of activities in all the new member states has resulted in a parallel rise over recent years in the number of signatures and ratifications of Charter instruments.

The activities carried out on the European Social Charter include seminars, study visits, as well as the production and distribution of documents and translations.

1. Seminars

Information and technical seminars

Meetings have already been organised in many member states. The aim of the ADACS activities concerning the Charter is to prepare countries for ratification. The first stage therefor consists of organising, in co-operation with the competent national authorities, an information seminar for civil servants of the country concerned, social partners, NGOs and academics. Parliamentarians are also involved in the seminars. Objectives are to explain the substance of the rights guaranteed and the functioning of the supervisory mechanism. The second stage consists of constructing compatibility studies of national legislation and practice with the Charter's norms.

Seminars for the preparation of first reports

Once states have ratified the Charter or the revised Charter, this activity is designed to help them compile their first national report on the implementation of the Charter or the revised Charter, to be submitted to the Committee of Independent Experts. The aim is to ensure that the first report contains the necessary information to allow the Committee to assess whether the country concerned fulfils its obligations under the Charter.

2. Study visits

These are organised either at the Council of Europe or within the administration of Contracting Parties, for civil servants of member states preparing to ratify the Charter, in order to examine Contracting Parties' legislation and the operation of the system of supervision (drafting of reports, follow-up of the supervision and other Charter-related matters). These visits allow officials to familiarise themselves with the Council of Europe and the Charter, with the operation of the supervisory system and their role as members of the Governmental Committee, as well as their responsibility for drafting the reports.

3. Documents and translations

The programme also involves providing documentation on fundamental social rights and translating and disseminating the texts of the Charter, its Protocols and the revised Charter, as well as documents relating to these treaties (basic texts and case law, etc.).

Each year in September-October, states are invited to submit their requests for the following year. The proposals retained are included in the budget-programme adopted by the Committee of Ministers.

Part C

Summary of the case law of the European Committee of Social Rights

Article 1 – The right to work

The right to work occupies a central place in the Social Charter, not only because it is important in its own right, but also because the actual exercise of several basic rights enshrined in this instrument is inconceivable unless the right to work is guaranteed first.

However, the right to work, as the Charter employs the term, does not mean that the state must guarantee a job to everyone who wants one, as any such provision would clearly be unworkable. The supply of jobs depends on the state of the labour market and on whether job-seekers' skills match its needs. Article 1, para. 1 of the Charter requires Contracting Parties to make full employment the primary objective of their economic policy. Paragraphs 2 to 4 contain three more specific obligations.

Paragraph 1 – Full employment

Under the first paragraph of Article 1 of the Charter, Contracting Parties undertake "to accept as one of their primary aims and respon-sibilities the achievement and maintenance of as high and stable a level of employment as possible, with a view to the attainment of full employment".

States must pursue an economic policy geared to achievement of this goal, ie. full employment: they must take measures for this purpose, and their reports must give the European Committee of Social Rights enough information to assess those measures' impact.

During the eighth supervision cycle, the Committee decided that it would adopt no further conclusions on this paragraph, ie. would give no further assessments on the conformity of national situations with it. However, it still reviews measures taken and policies implemented for the purpose of achieving full employment.

In doing so, it looks at various parameters, such as the proportion of economically active persons, the breakdown of employment by sector, by gender, between full-time and part-time contracts, and by contract type (permanent, fixed-term, etc.), trends in the nature of employment, the situation of the most vulnerable groups on the labour market (women, young people, long-term unemployed, immigrants from ethnic minorities), measures taken to help people in these groups to find jobs, and trends in total spending on employment policy, broken down by measures or programmes, with information on the relative shares of "active" measures (job creation, training, etc.) and "passive" measures (financial compensation, etc.) in total expenditure.

Paragraph 2 – The right of the worker to earn his living in an occupation freely entered upon

Under this paragraph, Contracting Parties undertake "to protect effectively the right of the worker to earn his living in an occupation freely entered upon".

The Committee has interpreted this provision as meaning that discrimination in employment must be eliminated, and forced labour prohibited.

A. *Elimination of discrimination in employment*

Article 1 para. 2 requires Contracting Parties to eliminate all forms of discrimination in employment.

To comply with Article 1 para. 2 in the matter of male/female equality, Parties must remove all the legal obstacles which deny women access to certain types of employment. They must also adopt legislation prohibiting discrimination between men and women in the workplace. This does not necessarily have to be specific: general legislation suffices. This prohibition must be backed by a number of safeguards: any clause in a collective agreement or individual contract which violates the principle of equality must be open to annulment, and sanctions must exist, and be applied, if discrimination occurs in practice. Dismissal for demanding equal treatment must also be prohibited, and anyone dismissed for this reason should normally be reinstated.

Article 1 of the Additional Protocol (No. 1), which is exclusively concerned with discrimination on grounds of gender, imposes more obligations on states than Article 1 para. 2.

Article 1 para. 2 also prohibits discrimination on other grounds, such as trade union membership, race, colour, religion, political opinion, national origin, membership of an ethnic minority, social origin and health.

B. *Prohibition of forced labour*

The forms of forced labour identified by the Committee mainly concern the merchant navy and aviation. For example, laws providing for criminal sanctions for merchant seamen who refuse to rejoin their ship, or to obey certain orders, are incompatible with the Charter. The Committee does recognise, however, that criminal sanctions are justified when the action in question endangers, or is liable to endanger, either the safety of the ship or the lives and health of those on board. Some states found guilty of violating this principle argue that their laws have fallen into disuse, but the Committee takes the view that the mere existence of such provisions constitutes a breach of Article 1 para. 2 since, as long as a law remains on the statute book, there is always a possibility that it will be applied.

Other situations have also been declared incompatible with the prohibition on forced labour: unduly long periods of military service with no possibility of leaving, criminal sanctions for requisitioned public servants, or people accused of deliberate idleness or of lacking the means of subsistence through their own fault.

Paragraph 3 – Free employment services

Under this paragraph, Contracting Parties undertake: "to establish or maintain free employment services for all workers".

This provision requires them to establish employment services and ensure that these operate effectively throughout their national territory. The main function of such services is to place job-seekers in employment.

Free placement services must be provided for both employees and employers.

Fee-based private services are not prohibited, provided that free services also exist in all sectors of the economy.

To determine the real effectiveness of state-run employment services, the Committee looks in particular at the number of placements made, the number of vacancies, and the respective market shares of public and private services. If not enough placements are being made, then the Charter is not being respected.

Finally, Article 1 para. 3 requires both sides of industry to participate in organising and running employment services.

Paragraph 4 – Vocational guidance, training and rehabilitation

Under this paragraph, Contracting Parties undertake "to provide or promote appropriate vocational guidance, training and rehabilitation".

Article 1 para. 4 embodies a general requirement. Since Article 1 is designed to ensure that effective exercise of the right to work is really guaranteed, paragraph 4 obliges states to provide vocational guidance and training services, as well as retraining, and to ensure access to these services for all interested persons, including nationals of other Charter states and the disabled.

Article 1 para. 4 is amplified by Articles 9, 10 and 15, which contain more detailed obligations relating to vocational guidance and training (see Fact Sheets C – 9, C – 10 and C – 15).

Information which national reports must include

First report

Answer all the questions on the Form for Reports.

In addition:

– for paragraph 1: answer the general question which appears in Conclusions XIV-1 (pp. 33-35);

– for paragraph 3: indicate the number of placements made by the employment services and the number of vacancies notified, and give figures for the market shares of the state employment services.

Subsequent reports

Report any changes during the reference period.

If some figures are hard to establish, give estimates based on valid, clearly defined methods.

Article 2 – The right to just conditions of work

Paragraph 1 – Reasonable working hours

The purpose of Article 2 para. 1 of the Social Charter, which is to "protect workers' health and safety – hence their lives", is directly related to the right to life.

To satisfy this provision, states must set reasonable limits on daily and weekly working time through legislation, regulations, collective agreements or any other binding means. An appropriate authority must supervise these measures, to ensure that the limits are respected in practice.

Normal hours and overtime must both be counted when working time is being calculated. Overtime must be regulated to ensure that it is not simply left to the discretion of the employer or the worker; the reasons for, and length of, overtime must be limited.

"Reasonable" daily and weekly working hours have not been defined in general terms: what may be considered reasonable under the Charter varies from place to place and from time to time.

There are, however, some situations which are not reasonable within the meaning of Article 2 para. 1, whatever the time or place: for example, to be considered reasonable under the Charter, working hours must never exceed sixteen hours a day or sixty hours a week.

In recent years, many states have adopted regulations providing for flexible working hours, ie. an arrangement which spreads them over a period longer than a week. These measures are not, in themselves, incompatible with the Charter.

The compatibility of these flexible schemes with Article 2, para. 1 depends on a number of factors :

a. The maximum daily and weekly hours referred to above must never be exceeded.

b. Flexible working hour schemes must have a basis in law. When they are covered by collective agreements, the Committee of Social Rights ascertains at what level those agreements have been signed. Additional safeguards are required when flexible working hours are provided for in collective agreements concluded within firms.

c. The reference periods used in calculating average working hours must not exceed four to six months; periods of up to one year may also be acceptable in exceptional circumstances.

d. In order to protect their private and family life, workers must be informed clearly and in good time of any changes in their working hours.

e. Appropriate protection must be provided for part-time workers, and temporaries "on call" or working discontinuous hours.

f. The Committee also looks at the way in which the Labour Inspectorate checks compliance with regulations and agreements on working hours.

Article 33 applies to this provision: this means that the right enshrined in Article 2 para. 1 must be enjoyed by at least 80% of workers. However, any law failing to satisfy the above criteria, and potentially applying to all workers, is – even if it affects less than 20% in practice – in breach of paragraph 1.

Article 2 para. 1 also requires Contracting Parties to reduce weekly working hours progressively, to the extent permitted by productivity increases and other relevant factors. These "other factors" may be the nature of the work and the safety and health risks to which workers are exposed. Under Article 2 para. 1, this obligation is closely related to the reasonable nature or otherwise of working time. The widespread introduction of the forty-hour week has thus greatly reduced the need to shorten the working week.

Paragraph 2 – Public holidays with pay

Contracting Parties must "provide for public holidays with pay", in addition to weekly rest periods and annual leave. These public holidays may be specified in law or in collective agreements.

The plural term, "public holidays", means there must be more than one, but the Committee has never specified a minimum number. The number of paid public holidays mentioned in the national reports has always been judged consistent with Article 2 para. 2; it currently ranges from six to seventeen days per year.

Working on public holidays is permitted in special cases; the conditions governing weekly rest periods (see below) apply, and the persons concerned must receive a compensatory rest period of equal duration or longer.

Article 33 applies to this provision: this means that the right enshrined in Article 2 para. 1 must be enjoyed by at least 80% of workers. However, any law failing to satisfy the above criteria, and potentially applying to all workers, is – even if it affects less than 20% in practice – in breach of paragraph 2.

Paragraph 3 – Annual holidays with pay

States must provide for a minimum of two weeks' annual holiday with pay.

Annual leave may not be replaced by financial compensation, and employees must not be free to forgo their annual leave.

It is permissible to require workers to be employed for twelve months before they become eligible for annual paid leave.

Workers who suffer illness or injury during their annual leave are entitled, on production of a medical certificate, to take the days lost at another time, so that they receive the two-week annual holiday provided for in the Charter.

Article 33 applies to this provision: this means that the right enshrined in Article 2 para. 3 must be enjoyed by at least 80% of workers. However, any law failing to satisfy the above criteria, and potentially applying to all workers, is – even if it affects less than 20% in practice – in breach of paragraph 3.

Paragraph 4 – Reduced working hours or additional paid holidays for workers in dangerous or unhealthy occupations

States are required to draw up a list of dangerous or unhealthy occupations and submit it to the Committee for inspection.

Sectors such as mining, quarrying, steel-making and ship-building have always been regarded as dangerous or unhealthy and remain so, but there are also new types of dangerous or unhealthy activity and new hazards – eg. ionising radiation, extreme temperatures, noise, working on computer screens, etc. Scientific progress has engendered new dangerous or unhealthy activities, and it has also revealed certain illness or risk factors, such as stress, which were previously disregarded.

Some states prefer to eliminate risks at source, instead of shortening working hours or granting extra holidays. Any blanket reduction in working time clearly applies to persons working in dangerous or unhealthy sectors too, so further reductions may well seem unnecessary. However, the Committee takes the view that, in sectors where risks cannot be entirely eliminated, shorter working hours must be imposed or extra leave granted. Merely reducing exposure to risks is not enough to satisfy Article 2 para. 4 – and nor are higher wages or bonuses, in the absence of other measures.

125

Article 33 applies to this provision, but the phrase "the great majority of the workers concerned" (80%) means the majority of workers in dangerous or unhealthy occupations, and not all workers.

Paragraph 5 – Weekly rest period

Article 2 para. 5 requires states to do two things: to guarantee a weekly rest period, and to ensure, whenever possible, that it coincides with the day traditionally or normally recognised as a day of rest in the country or region concerned, ie. Sunday in all the states which have so far ratified the Charter.

Weekly rest periods may not be replaced by compensation and workers may not forego them.

The rest period must be "weekly", but the Committee allows it to be deferred, provided that no one works more than twelve consecutive days without a two-day rest period.

Sunday working is permitted in special circumstances: the persons concerned must receive a compensatory rest period of equal duration or longer.

Information which national reports must include

First report

As well as answering the questions on the Form for Reports, state whether there are any regulations on working time adjustments and, if so, describe them (laws or collective agreements).

For paragraphs 2, 3 and 5, indicate:
– the occupations and the number of people concerned;
– the permitted derogations;
– how these provisions are applied to part-time workers.

Subsequent reports

Report any changes during the reference period, and particularly the introduction of any working time adjustment schemes (indicating how they are applied in practice).

FACT SHEET C – 3

Article 3 – The right to safe and healthy working conditions

Article 3 of the Social Charter, which requires Contracting Parties to guarantee the right to safe and healthy working conditions, protects the individual's right to physical and mental well-being at work. Its purpose is related to the right to life.

Paragraph 1 – Safety and health regulations

The regulations must provide for preventive and protective measures against most of the risks specified in the international technical reference standards, ie. the ILO Conventions and the Community directives on health and safety at work.

These preventive and protective measures must apply with no major omissions: all workers – employed and self-employed alike – must be protected, regardless of their occupational category and sector of activity. Other crucial factors are: the degree of precision of the regulations, the relative importance of the occupations concerned in the national economy and hence the number of people involved, and the extent to which the regulations reflect current knowledge, as established by international reference standards.

In addition to framework legislation, imposing general obligations on employers and workers, states must also introduce regulations providing for measures to combat risks and hazards in a number of areas, which can vary with change, particularly technical change, and are currently as follows :

a. Workplaces – work equipment:

- protection of machines;
- manual handling of loads;
- maximum weight;
- air pollution, noise and vibration;
- personal protective equipment;

- safety and/or health signs at work;
- display screens.

b. Hazardous agents and substances:
- chemical, physical and biological agents, including white lead (painting), benzene, asbestos and ionising radiation.

c. Risks connected with certain sectors or activities:
- dock work;
- building industry;
- mining and extracting industries;
- ships and fishing vessels;
- prevention of major industrial accidents.

d. Risks connected with certain vulnerable categories of worker:[1]

Persons in insecure jobs (temporary or fixed-term employment and self-employment) are exposed to cumulative health and safety risks, owing both to the nature of the work they are offered (often in the building and industrial sectors) and to their status. Special rules are therefore needed to ensure that they enjoy the same level of health protection at work as other workers.

e. Specific risks

i. Asbestos

- Maximum exposure levels

ILO Convention No. 162 and Community Directive 83/477, amended by Directive 91/382, require exposure to asbestos to be reduced to the lowest possible levels and provide for exposure limits. The Directive sets these limits at 0.6 fibres per cm3 for chrysolite (ribbon fibres, which are not considered particularly dangerous) and at 0.3 fibres per cm3 for other types of asbestos. Under the ILO Convention, limits must be regularly reviewed and updated to keep pace with developments in science and technology.

To satisfy Article 3, para. 1, exposure limits must be equal to or lower than those laid down in the Directive.

- Prohibition measures

The ILO Convention and the Directive prohibit all forms of asbestos spraying. The ILO Convention also requires that, when this is necessary and technically feasible, the law should provide

---

1. Article 7 of the Charter contains provisions on special measures to protect the health and safety of children and adolescents in cases where they are permitted to work (see Fact Sheet C – 7).
Under Article 8, para. 4 of the Charter, the employment of women on industrial night work must be regulated, and the employment of women on underground mining work and, when appropriate, on all other work unsuited to them by reason of its dangerous, unhealthy or arduous nature must be prohibited (see Fact Sheet C - 8).

for replacement of asbestos by other less toxic materials, or should partly or wholly prohibit the use of asbestos. At all events, the use of one of the most harmful forms of asbestos (crocidolite) must be prohibited.

Article 3 does not require that asbestos be totally prohibited, although the Committee takes the view that this would ensure more effective protection of the right provided for in Article 3, para. 1.

– In addition, steps must be taken to draw up an inventory of all contaminated buildings and materials.

II. Ionising radiation

The maximum levels laid down in 1990 by the International Commission on Protection against Radiation must be respected.

Paragraph 2 – Supervision of the enforcement of safety and health regulations

The Committee monitors compliance with this requirement, taking account of trends in industrial accidents and diseases, and of the introduction and maintenance of effective inspection arrangements.

a. Industrial accidents and diseases

The Committee takes account of the total number and incidence (number per hundred workers) of injuries. If the report does not provide all the information it needs, it consults ILO or Eurostat figures.

In cases where there is an obvious problem, it concludes that Article 3 para. 2 is not being respected.

b. Activities of the Labour Inspectorate

The Committee takes account of the number of firms supervised by the Inspectorate, the number of workers employed by those firms, the number of inspections carried out and the number of workers covered by those inspections. It believes that maintaining an effective inspection system depends on carrying out a minimum number of regular inspections, for the purpose of ensuring that the right enshrined in Article 3 is effectively enjoyed by a maximum number of workers.

The inspectors must have power to use coercive measures if they find that there is an immediate danger to the health or safety of workers. The Committee also checks to see whether sanctions for employers are sufficiently deterrent.

Paragraph 3 – Consultation with employers' and workers' organisations on questions of safety and health

The obligation to consult the social partners applies to all sectors of the economy, including the public sector. Consultation must focus on measures to improve industrial safety and health, and take place whenever the need arises, particularly in response to changes in the regulations.

Contracting Parties must ensure that machinery and procedures for consultation between professional organisations and the public authorities exist at national level. The body set up for this purpose may be either a permanent or an ad hoc consultation body. Consultation at regional level is necessary only when warranted by geography.

The professional organisations must also be consulted at enterprise level.

Information which national reports must include

First report

In answering the questions on the Form for Reports, list the main laws and regulations currently in force on health and safety at work, clearly indicating their scope (material and personal).

Describe the system of labour inspection and sanctions, enclosing copies of reports submitted to the ILO on the activities of the labour inspectorates (firms inspected and workers employed by those firms, inspections carried out and workers covered by those inspections), on violations and on sanctions imposed.

Finally, describe the machinery for consultation of the social partners at national and enterprise level, and provide information on practice in this area.

Subsequent reports

Report any changes during the reference period, particularly changes in laws and regulations. Give figures for the number of industrial accidents and diseases during the reference period.

Article 4 – The right to a fair remuneration

Article 4 of the Social Charter contains a number of basic guarantees concerning wages and wage protection, which supplement the other employment protection standards set out in Articles 1 to 3. The principle of fairness underlies each of these guarantees, particularly where wage levels are concerned.

Paragraph 1 – Fair remuneration

This provision guarantees a fair wage: to be considered fair within the meaning of Article 4 para. 1, a wage must not fall too far short of the national average. The threshold adopted by the Committee is 60% (net value). Also, wages must always be above the poverty line in the country concerned.

The remuneration taken into account, for the purposes of this provision, is the remuneration – either monetary or in kind – paid by an employer to a worker for work done. Account is also taken, where applicable, of special bonuses and gratuities.

The Committee's calculations are based on net amounts, ie. after deduction of social security contributions, and allowing for any income tax relief to which the worker may be entitled. Social transfers (eg. social security allowances or benefits) are taken into account only when they are directly linked to the wage.

The net national average wage of a full-time worker is calculated with reference to the labour market as a whole, or at least representative sectors, such as the manufacturing or service industries. When a national minimum wage exists, its net amount is used as a basis for comparison with the net average wage. Otherwise, the minimum wage determined by collective agreement or the lowest wage actually paid provides the yardstick.

A net wage which falls below the 60% threshold is not automatically considered unfair within the meaning of the Charter. If it lies between 60 and 50%, a state may be asked to show that it suffices to give the worker a decent standard of living, eg. by providing detailed information on the cost of living. However, a net wage which is less than half the net national average counts as unfair and thus incompatible with Article 4 para. 1.

Paragraph 2 – Increased remuneration for overtime work

This paragraph is intrinsically connected with Article 2 para. 1, which concerns daily and weekly working time. Workers required to do overtime must be paid above the normal hourly rate. The Committee has not specified what the minimum increase must be.

Leave may be granted to compensate for overtime, but must be longer than the overtime worked. In other words, it is not enough to give the person concerned leave equal to the number of extra hours worked.

This provision applies to all workers, except "in particular cases". The Committee has indicated that these exceptions, which may apply to certain categories of civil servant and executive, must be few and far between.

The Committee recently looked at the impact of flexible working hours on remuneration for overtime. The general tendency in Europe is to calculate working hours by taking a weekly average over a period of several months. During this period, the number of hours actually worked in any week may vary between a maximum and a minimum figure, without there being any question of overtime, and thus a higher rate of remuneration. Arrangements of this kind do not, in themselves, violate Article 4 para. 2, provided that the conditions laid down in Article 2 para. 1 are respected (see Fact Sheet C – 2).

Paragraph 3 – Equal pay for women and men

The right of male and female workers to equal pay for work of equal value must be expressly provided for in domestic law.

This applies to all work of equal value, which means that comparisons may not be confined to any one job or firm, but must be possible with other jobs and other firms.

National law must provide that all clauses in employment contracts or collective agreements which violate the principle of equal pay are null and void. A court must have power to annul them.

Employees who claim their right to equal pay must be legally protected against reprisals by employers. Dismissals on this ground are prohibited. Employees subjected to reprisals must receive compensation sufficient not only to make good the damage, but also to deter the employer from taking such action in future. Compensation for dismissal should normally take the form of reinstatement. In exceptional circumstances, it may take the form of a payment if reinstatement is impossible, or the person concerned does not wish it.

Paragraph 4 – Reasonable notice of termination of employment

This provision is included in the Article on remuneration, as the main purpose of reasonable notice is to give the person concerned time to look for work before his current employment ends, ie. while he is still earning. This is why wages in lieu of notice are permissible, provided that the sum paid is equivalent to that which the worker would have earned during a reasonable period within the meaning of the Charter.

The right to reasonable notice of termination of employment applies to all categories of employee, including those employed on a non-standard basis. It also applies to persons on probation. National law must be broad enough to ensure that no workers are left unprotected.

The Committee has never defined "reasonable" notice in general terms, but has merely indicated what periods of notice it considers unreasonable. Its chief criterion – which is also decisive in most countries' law – is length of service. It has ruled, for example, that the following are incompatible with the Charter:
– one week's notice during the first year of service;
– less than one month's notice after one year of service;
– thirty days' notice after at least five years' service;
– six weeks' notice after ten to fifteen years' service;
– eight weeks' notice after more than fifteen years' service.

The Committee considers that regulations providing for shorter notice for young workers are unjustified.

Procedures which delay a decision to terminate employment (eg. disciplinary proceedings in the civil service or trade union consultation) are excluded from the period of notice, which starts only when the decision has been taken.

Article 4 para. 4 does not apply solely to dismissals, but to all cases of termination of employment (due, for example, to bankruptcy, invalidity or death of the employer).

The Appendix to the Charter permits immediate dismissal (ie. without notice) in cases of serious misconduct – but this exception must be interpreted very strictly.

Workers must be given time off to look for a new job during the period of notice.

Information which national reports must include

First report

Answer all the questions on the Form for Reports.

Under Article 4 para. 2, describe the arrangements for adjusting working time (if not already done under Article 2 para. 1).

Subsequent reports

Report any changes during the reference period.

Provide figures on wages for each year of the reference period.

Article 5 – The right to organise

Article 5 of the Social Charter guarantees the right of workers and employers to organise.

This right covers several areas:

1. Freedom to form trade unions

a. *Requirements concerning registration and dues, minimum membership and other administrative requirements*

Compulsory registration is not incompatible with Article 5, provided that:

- there are adequate safeguards to ensure that the power to refuse to register trade unions is not misused;
- registration fees are reasonable;
- minimum membership requirements are also set at a reasonable level.

b. *Right of a trade union to choose its members and representatives*

The following are not compatible with Article 5:

- any law restricting the grounds on which trade unions may exclude or expel individuals, since this greatly reduces their freedom to choose their own members;
- any law making eligibility to serve as a trade union representative conditional on nationality or residence.

c. *Right of a trade union to organise its own activities and internal management*

Trade unions must be free to manage their own affairs without government interference. Any law containing detailed regulations on their internal operations poses a serious risk of interference and is thus incompatible with Article 5.

135

d. *Membership*

Workers and employers must be free to form local, national or international organisations. This means that states may not limit the level on which workers are permitted to organise. They must also allow national organisations to join international organisations.

2. **Right to join or not to join a trade union**

The law (or case law) must guarantee or protect the right to join a trade union, and people must be totally free in practice to join the union of their choice.

The same applies to the right not to join, which must be enshrined in law (or case law) and respected in practice. Any form of compulsory union membership, imposed by law, is incompatible with the Charter. Closed-shop agreements (before or after hiring) are also incompatible with Article 5. States must not have legislation authorising such practices, or allow them to exist.

3. **Trade union activities**

a. *Collective bargaining*

This right is a fundamental trade union prerogative, and is recognised in Articles 5 and 6 of the Charter.

b. *Access to the workplace and right of assembly*

Trade unions' right of access to firms for the purpose of exercising their activities is guaranteed by Article 5, on the understanding that account must taken of the rights and interests of employers.

c. *Protection against anti-trade union discrimination and reprisals for trade union activity*

Under Article 5, workers must be protected in law and in fact against all discrimination in respect of recruitment, dismissal and promotion on grounds of trade union membership or activity.

4. **Persons protected by Article 5 (personal scope)**

a. *Civil servants*

Article 5 prohibits special restrictions on the right of civil servants to organise. States may not restrict this right, for example, by allowing them to join only trade unions with an exclusively civil service membership. However, under Article 31 of the Charter, some restrictions on the freedom of association of certain categories of civil servant are compatible with Article 5.[1]

---

1. The effective exercise of the rights and principles set forth in Part II may not "be subject to any restrictions or limitations not specified in those parts, except such as are prescribed by law and are necessary in a democratic society for the protection of the rights and freedoms of others or for the protection of public interest, national security, public health, or morals".

b. Police

Article 5 allows Contracting Parties to restrict police officers' right to organise, but not to abolish it completely. Police officers may be allowed to join or form only organisations with an exclusively police membership. These organisations must be able, however, to exercise certain trade union prerogatives, such as the right to negotiate conditions of service and remuneration and the right of assembly. Membership may not be made compulsory.

c. Armed forces

Article 5 allows Contracting Parties to restrict, or even do away with, the freedom of association of members of the armed forces.

d. Foreigners

Under the Appendix, the Charter applies only to foreigners who are nationals of other Charter states, living or working lawfully in the state concerned. Restrictions on foreigners who are officials or founding members of trade unions have been ruled incompatible with Article 5. A situation in which a collective agreement required trade union officials to hold a certain nationality was also ruled incompatible with Article 5. This aspect of Article 5 is closely connected with Article 19 para. 4b, which requires Contracting Parties – where trade union membership and enjoyment of the benefits of collective bargaining are concerned – to secure for migrant workers treatment no less favourable than that accorded their own nationals.

Information which national reports must include

First report

Answer all the questions on the Form for Reports. Also provide information on subjects dealt with in sections 1 to 4 above.

Subsequent reports

Report any changes in law or practice during the reference period.

Article 6 – The right to bargain collectively

Article 6 of the Social Charter guarantees the right to bargain collectively in the broad sense.

This Article is designed to ensure that both employers and employees have the right to bargain collectively. Its four paragraphs cover various aspects of relations between employers and workers, and between their organisations, as well as the means which should be used to develop those relations.

Paragraph 1 – Joint consultation

The obligation set out in Article 6 para. 1 is to promote joint consultation. If consultation is already adequate, there will thus be no need for the state to intervene. If it is not, however, the state must take steps to encourage it.

The joint consultation in question is consultation between employees and employers, or the organisations that represent them. Article 6 para. 1 does not apply to consultation between governments and employees and/or employers or their organisations. However, consultation which takes place within a body, chaired by government, on which workers and employers are equally represented, is deemed to satisfy Article 6 para. 1.

Consultation must cover all matters of mutual interest, and particularly: productivity, efficiency, industrial health, safety and welfare, and other occupational issues (working conditions, vocational training, etc.), economic problems and social matters (social insurance, social welfare, etc.).

It must take place on several levels: national, regional and within firms.

Article 6 para. 1 applies not only to private sector employees, but also – with the necessary adjustments – to civil servants, including those covered by special regulations.

Paragraph 2 – Voluntary negotiation

Paragraph 2 requires Contracting Parties not only to recognise in their legislation that employers and workers may regulate their relations by collective agreement, but also to promote the conclusion of such agreements when they do not evolve naturally, and particularly to ensure that each side is prepared to bargain collectively with the other.

Under Article 6 para. 2 the Committee reviews state intervention in collective bargaining and the use of compulsory arbitration: direct state action to end collective bargaining, eg. by imposing arbitration without the parties' consent, is permissible only within the limits prescribed by Article 31 of the Charter.[1] Moreover, such action must be taken for the time needed to restore a normal situation, in which the right to bargain collectively is again fully exercised.

Article 6 para. 2 is closely related to Article 5. When a question relating to collective bargaining arises under Article 5 and the Committee's conclusion is negative or deferred, the same conclusion applies to Article 6 para. 2.

Article 6 para. 2 also applies – with the necessary adjustments – to civil servants. In particular, civil servants must have some say in determining their working conditions.

Paragraph 3 – Conciliation and arbitration

Article 6 para. 3 – like Article 6 para. 4 – applies only to conflicts of interest. In other words, it does not apply to legal disputes (concerning, for example, the interpretation of collective agreements) or to political disputes.

Conciliation and arbitration procedures may be instituted by law, collective agreement or industrial practice. When, for example, the conciliation machinery established by collective agreement is sufficiently effective, government has no need to bring in such procedures.

All arbitration systems must be independent, and the outcome of arbitration may not be predetermined by legislative criteria.

Compulsory arbitration is also covered by Article 6 para. 3. The use of arbitration procedures without the consent of the parties may be considered compatible with the Charter only within the limits prescribed by Article 31.

---

1. The rights and principles set forth in Part II may not "be subject to any restrictions or limitations not specified in those parts, except such as are prescribed by law and are necessary in a democratic society for the protection of the rights and freedoms of others or for the protection of public interest, national security, public health, or morals".

Conciliation and arbitration procedures must also be instituted in the civil service.

Paragraph 4 – Collective action

Article 6 para. 4 guarantees the right of workers and employers to take collective action, including strike action. The right to strike is expressly mentioned, but is only one of the types of action which workers may take.

Paragraph 4 permits collective action only in cases of conflicts of interest.

Even in cases of conflicts of interest, however, the right to strike is not absolute; states may regulate its exercise, provided that any restrictions fall within the limits prescribed by Article 31 of the Charter.

The Committee has had occasion to examine the following restrictions and regulations:

- periods of notice or cooling-off periods, prescribed by law in connection with pre-strike conciliation procedures, are compatible with the Charter, but must be of reasonable duration;
- restrictions on the right to strike imposed by collective agreements are compatible with Article 6 para. 4, provided that they apply only to matters covered, and workers bound, by the agreement in question;
- the requirement that the purpose of striking must be to conclude a collective agreement is not compatible with Article 6 para. 4;
- the requirement that strikes must be called or led by trade unions also violates Article 6 para. 4;
- restricting the right to strike of certain categories of public servant (eg. police, armed forces, judiciary) is not incompatible with the Charter, provided that these restrictions fall within the limits prescribed by Article 31. However, totally prohibiting public servants from striking is incompatible with Article 6, para. 4;
- legislation which denies persons employed in essential public services the right to strike, either totally or partially, may be compatible with the Charter, provided that this restriction falls within the limits prescribed by Article 31.

The effects of a strike are also important under Article 6 para. 4. If striking results in termination of the employment contract, then this is not compatible with Article 6 para. 4. In practice, however, if strikers are fully reinstated when the strike has ended, and their previously acquired entitlements (eg. concerning pensions, holidays and seniority) are not impaired, then formal termination of the employment contract does not violate the Charter.

Any deductions from strikers' wages must be proportional to the duration of the strike.

When governments intervene, using legislation or compulsory arbitration to end strikes, the Committee examines each case on its merits, in order to see whether Article 31 has actually been respected.

Lockout

Article 6 para. 4 also recognises the right of employers to take collective action, which normally takes the form of a lockout. States are not obliged, however, to establish full legal equality between the right to strike and the right to order a lockout.

Information which national reports must include

First report

Answer all the questions on the Form for Reports.

For Article 6 para. 4, provide in addition the following information:

a. Meaning of collective action; what forms of action are recognised?

b. Permissible aims of collective action: when and to what extent is collective action safeguarded?

c. Who is entitled to take collective action?

d. Restrictions on the right to take collective action.

e. Consequences of collective action.

f. Procedural requirements relating to collective action.

Subsequent reports

Report any changes in law or practice during the reference period.

Article 7 – Rights of children – protection of young people

Article 7 of the Social Charter prohibits the employment of children (paras. 1, 2 and 3) and regulates various aspects of working conditions for young people (paras. 4, 5, 6, 7, 8 and 9). The aim is to protect their health and their right to enjoy the full benefits of compulsory schooling and vocational training.

Article 7 para. 10 also stipulates that children and young people must be protected against physical and moral dangers, particularly, but not exclusively in the work environment (see Fact Sheet C – 17).

Paragraph 1 – Prohibition of child labour

Contracting Parties are required to set the minimum age of admission to employment at fifteen years, and to make sure that this age limit is respected in practice.

This applies to all fields of activity, ie. all economic sectors and all types of firm, including family businesses, and to all types of work, remunerated or otherwise, including agricultural work, housework, work in the home, sub-contracting and work in the family context.

The only exception to the ban on employment of children under the age of fifteen permitted by paragraph 1 is prescribed light work which is not likely to harm their health, morals or education.

In principle, a restrictive list of such authorised work must be drawn up. States who have no lists of authorised or prohibited work must define "light work" exactly in their laws or regulations.

Work regarded as "light" *per se* ceases to be so when the hours worked are too long.

143

Paragraph 2 – Higher minimum age of admission to certain occupations

For dangerous or unhealthy work, Contracting Parties must set a minimum age of admission to employment higher than fifteen years. Each state must decide which work is dangerous or unhealthy and draw up a list. The Committee checks this list for omissions in the light, *inter alia,* of accident-at-work statistics for young people.

When listing dangerous or unhealthy occupations, states must determine the ages at which young people may be admitted to them without undue risk to their health.

The minimum age for work involving exposure to benzene must not be lower than eighteen.

Paragraph 3 – Right to the full benefit of compulsory education

This provision prohibits the employment of children still undergoing compulsory schooling[1] on any work which would prevent them from benefiting fully from their education.

Light work is the only kind that does not prevent such children from benefiting fully from their education. The "light work" permissible under Article 7 para. 3 is the same as that permissible under Article 7 para. 1.

Domestic law must specify the number of hours which schoolchildren may work. The Committee has set no general limit on hours permissible under this provision, but has identified situations which are not permissible, eg.:

- twenty to twenty-five hours' work a week during the school year;

- three hours' work on school days and six to eight hours on week days when there is no school;

- forty-nine hours of combined school and non-school work for children over thirteen years of age.

It is contrary to the Charter to authorise children to work before the school day begins; and rest periods – when no work is done – during school holidays must account for at least half of the holidays.

The Committee also considers that seven hours' work a day and thirty-five hours a week during school holidays is too much for fourteen- and fifteen-year-olds, and that eight hours a day and forty hours

---

1. Article 7 para. 1 concerns children from 0 to 15 years old. Article 7 para. 3 concerns children from the beginning to the end of compulsory schooling. For Contracting Parties which have accepted both provisions, the Committee examines the situation from 0 to 15 years of age with reference to paragraph 1, then from age 15 to the end of compulsory schooling with reference to paragraph 3.

a week during school holidays is too much for children over fifteen years of age.

Paragraph 4 – Working hours for under-sixteens

Contracting Parties must limit the hours worked by young people between the ages of fifteen and sixteen who are no longer in compulsory schooling.

The Committee has set no definite limit on hours worked under this provision, but regards any law which allows under-sixteens to work up to eight hours a day or forty hours a week as incompatible with paragraph 4.

Since Article 33 applies to Article 7 para. 4, states are held to honour their commitments if this provision applies to at least 80% of young workers under sixteen years of age.

Paragraph 5 – Fair remuneration for young workers and apprentices

Article 7 para. 5 requires Contracting Parties to recognise the right of young workers and apprentices to a fair wage or other appropriate allowances.

The Committee assesses this by comparing young workers' remuneration with the starting wage paid to adults (age eighteen or over).

The young worker's wage may be less than the adult starting wage, but the difference must be reasonable and the gap must close quickly. For fifteen/sixteen-year-olds, a wage 30% lower than the adult starting wage is acceptable under the Charter. For sixteen/eighteen-year-olds, the difference may not exceed 20%.

The adult reference wage must in any case be sufficient to comply with Article 4 para. 1 of the Charter. If the reference wage is too low, even a young worker's wage which respects these percentage differentials is not considered fair.

Apprentices may be paid lower wages, since the value of the on-the-job training they receive must be taken into account. However, the apprenticeship system must not be deflected from its purpose and be used to underpay young workers. Accordingly, apprenticeships should not last too long and, as skills are acquired, the allowance should be gradually increased throughout the contract period.

The sum paid to an apprentice should be at least one-third of the adult starting wage at the start of the apprenticeship, and at least two-thirds at the end.

Contracting Parties are not required to enact legislation in order to comply with paragraph 5, but they must be able to show that a network of collective agreements or some other arrangement guarantees that all young workers receive a fair wage, and apprentices an appropriate allowance.

Paragraph 6 – Time spent on vocational training treated as part of the working day

Time spent on vocational training by young people during normal working hours must be treated as part of the working day.

Such training must, in principle, be done with the employer's consent and be related to the young person's work.

Training time must thus be remunerated like normal working time, and there must be no obligation to make it up, which would effectively increase the total number of hours worked.

Since Article 33 applies to Article 7 para. 4, states are held to honour their commitment if this provision effectively applies, thanks to collective agreements or other non-legislative means, to at least 80% of the young people concerned.

Paragraph 7 – Paid annual holidays for under-eighteens

Workers under eighteen years of age must be given at least three weeks' annual holiday with pay.

The arrangements which apply are the same as those applying to annual paid leave for adults (Article 2 para. 3, see Fact Sheet C – 2).

Article 33 applies to paragraph 7, which may therefore be enforced by non-legislative means, provided that at least 80% of the young people concerned are covered.

Paragraph 8 – Prohibition of night work for under-eighteens

Contracting Parties must ensure that under-eighteens are not employed on night work, with the exception of certain occupations specified in national laws or regulations.

Under the Appendix, Contracting Parties may fulfil their obligation through legislation ensuring that the great majority of under-eighteens (at least 80%) are not employed on night work.

It is up to national laws or regulations to define "night work". The concept's meaning may vary with age groups and seasons.

A situation in which the ban on night work applies only to industrial work is incompatible with the Charter.

Paragraph 9 – Regular medical supervision for workers under eighteen

Contracting Parties must provide for compulsory regular medical check-ups for under-eighteens employed in occupations specified by national laws or regulations.

These check-ups must be adapted to the specific situation of young workers and the particular risks to which they are exposed. They may, however, be carried out by the general works medicine services, if they are specifically instructed to do so.

The obligation covers a full medical examination on recruitment and regular check-ups thereafter. The Committee has laid down no general rule on frequency, but has decided in certain cases – eg. young seamen required to have check-ups only every three years – that the intervals were too long.

These medical examinations must be compulsory and carried out in practice for all the workers concerned.

Paragraph 10 – Special protection for children and young people against physical and moral dangers to which they are exposed

Contracting Parties must protect children and young people against all the physical and moral dangers to which they are exposed, at work and elsewhere.

Contracting Parties must take special measures to protect children and young people working in certain sectors, particularly the arts, show business, advertising and the media. Protection must extend to alcohol and drug abuse, etc.

Protection outside work should focus, *inter alia,* on alcohol and drug abuse, and juvenile delinquency. It must extend to all forms of ill-treatment (including sexual abuse and ill-treatment within families, corporal punishment, etc.).

Finally, Contracting Parties must set up bodies to supervise application of the relevant domestic legal provisions.

Information which national reports must include

First report

Answer all the questions on the Form for Reports and describe the actual situation. Supply information on measures to supervise the application of legislation and on the actual situation.

Indicate the scope of each of the relevant texts.

Contracting Parties which have not accepted Article 4 para. 1 should provide, under Article 7 para. 5, enough information for the

Committee to compare the remuneration of young people and apprentices with adult starting wages.

For Article 7 para. 10, provide information on action taken to prevent alcohol and drug abuse and juvenile delinquency. Also provide information on the protection of children against all forms of ill-treatment (including sexual abuse and ill-treatment in families, corporal punishment, etc.).

Subsequent reports

Report any changes in law or practice during the reference period.

Article 8 – Rights related to maternity – conditions of employment for women

Article 8 of the Charter covers the right of pregnant women and recent or nursing mothers to protection, and also applies to night work and to dangerous, unhealthy or arduous work.

This provision applies to all women in paid employment, including civil servants. Only self-employed women are excluded.

Paragraph 1 – Maternity leave

Article 8 para. 1 imposes two obligations on Contracting Parties:

a. *The right to maternity leave*

The right to maternity leave must be guaranteed by law. Its minimum duration must be twelve weeks. It is a right, not an obligation, and women are free not to take it – but may not forego six weeks' compulsory leave immediately after childbirth.

b. *The right to cash benefits*

Article 8 para. 1 provides for twelve weeks' paid maternity leave, covered by social security benefits or from public funds, as Contracting Parties decide.

The amount paid must be as close as possible to the woman's former salary.

When payment takes the form of social security benefits and these are subject to a ceiling, that ceiling must be fixed at a reasonable level.

Paragraph 2 – Unlawful dismissal

Under Article 8 para. 2, employers may not give women notice of dismissal while on maternity leave, or at a time which would mean that notice expired during maternity leave.

Women are protected throughout the period of maternity leave to which they are entitled. The ban on notice of dismissal, expiring during absence on maternity leave, means that employment may not be terminated during that period. Consequently, legislation permitting the giving of notice of dismissal to a pregnant woman before, or even during, her maternity leave is not contrary to Article 8 para. 2, provided that dismissal does not take effect during such leave, and that periods of prior notice and any other procedures are suspended until it ends.

This rule is not absolute. It may be waived in certain circumstances: if the woman in question is guilty of misconduct warranting termination of her contract, or if the firm goes out of business.

This provision applies equally to women on fixed-term and open-ended contracts. The Committee makes sure that fixed-term contracts are not used to circumvent the ban on dismissal during maternity leave.

In cases of dismissal contravening this provision, reinstatement must be automatic. Exceptionally, if this is impossible or the woman concerned does not wish it, compensation must be paid. The sum must be sufficient both to deter the employer and compensate the victim of dismissal.

Paragraph 3 – Time off for nursing mothers

Under this paragraph, Contracting Parties undertake to give mothers who are nursing their babies time off for that purpose.

Time off for nursing must be treated as normal working time and remunerated as such.

The Committee has not specified the length of time off or the period during which it must be granted: it appraises each situation on its merits. None the less, it takes the view that time off should, by definition, be granted during working hours – and that provision for extended leave or part-time work is not enough to satisfy Article 8 para. 3.

Paragraph 4 – Regulation of night work and prohibition of dangerous, unhealthy and arduous work

a. Regulation of night work in industrial employment (Article 8 para. 4a)

This provision applies only to industrial work in the strict sense. In industry, there are also non-industrial jobs to which it does not apply:

– women in executive posts or technical posts carrying responsibilities;

– women working in health and welfare services, who are not usually required to do manual work.

Article 8 para. 4*a* requires Contracting Parties to regulate – not prohibit – night work for women. The regulations must:

- strictly control exceptions to the rules on night work, which must be authorised only when special production needs make them necessary, having due regard to working conditions and the organisation of work in the firm concerned;

- lay down conditions for night work, eg. prior authorisation by the Labour Inspectorate (when applicable), prescribed working hours, breaks, rest days following periods of night work, etc.

Special regulations on night work by women are not required, however, if the general regulations on night work provide the requisite protection.

b. *Strict prohibition on the employment of women in certain types of work (Article 8 para. 4b)*

Article 8 para. 4*b* prohibits two things:

- the employment of women on underground work in mines. This applies to extraction work proper, but not to women who:

  - occupy executive posts and do no manual work,

  - work in health and welfare services,

  - spend brief training periods in underground sections of mines.

This prohibition must be provided for in law.

- the employment of women, "in all other work which is unsuitable by reason of its dangerous, unhealthy or arduous nature"; the Committee has explained that this prohibition applies only when it is necessary, ie. to protect mothers, particularly during pregnancy, confinement and the post-natal period, and also unborn children.

Certain activities, such as those involving exposure to lead, benzene, ionising radiation, high temperatures, vibration or viral agents, must be covered.

Information which national reports must include

First report

Supply all the information asked for on the Form for Reports. In addition, supply information on the following:

Article 8 para. 1

- the duration of compulsory post-natal leave;

- any ceiling for benefits, its level, arrangements for reviewing it, and the number of women earning more than this ceiling;

- any conditions governing the payment of cash maternity benefits, eg. a certain period of insurance under a social security scheme, a certain period of occupational activity, or length of service (stating whether periods of unemployment are counted as time worked), and/or a particular wage level.

Article 8 para. 2

– authorised exceptions to the prohibition on dismissal during maternity leave, and action taken in cases of wrongful dismissal during maternity leave (reinstatement, compensation);

– applicability of this prohibition to women employed on fixed-term contracts.

Article 8 para. 3

– remuneration and duration of time off for nursing mothers.

Article 8 para. 4

– categories of women covered by the regulations on night work and the prohibition on types of work referred to in sub-paragraph b.

Subsequent reports

Report any changes in law or practice during the reference period.

Article 9 – The right to vocational guidance

Under Article 9 of the Charter, Contracting Parties undertake to provide or promote services to help all persons, including those with disabilities, to solve problems concerning occupational choice and progress. This assistance must be available free of charge, both to young people, including schoolchildren, and to adults.

Compliance with Article 9 is closely related to compliance with Article 1 on the right to work.

In order to guarantee a satisfactory level of skills and qualifications among the workforce, Contracting Parties must provide careers guidance within the school system (information on training and access to training) and within the labour market (training and retraining, taking account of job openings and trainees' desire to progress in their careers).

The Committee bases its assessment of Contracting Parties' compliance with this provision on various qualitative and quantitative criteria, eg.:

– the vocational guidance budget as a percentage of GDP;
– the number and qualifications of the specialised staff providing guidance;
– the geographical distribution of both types of guidance, which should be balanced;
– the type of information available and the means used to disseminate it, the aim being to reach as many people as possible;
– the number of people who receive guidance, as well as their ages and educational/training background.

Article 9 also requires that vocational guidance be provided free of charge.

As in the rest of the Charter, the key principle here is equal opportunity for all. Article 9 is based solely on the criterion of individual ability, with no discrimination whatsoever.

The Committee accordingly looks at the efforts made by Contracting Parties to ensure gender equality in their guidance and training services, and at programmes to ensure that people with disabilities have access to these services. Another aspect of non-discrimination is the obligation to ensure that nationals of one Contracting Party, lawfully residing or working in another, receive exactly the same treatment as home nationals.

Information which national reports must include

First report

Answer all the questions on the Form for Reports and:

– describe the structure of vocational guidance services in detail, indicating their geographical distribution. Specify whether they are free of charge;

– state the number of people employed, their training and qualifications, and also the type of assistance provided (eg. individual, collective, self-service, computer-assisted, etc.) and the groups covered;

– describe the situation of traditionally vulnerable groups and action taken to give them equal access to guidance;

– explain how equal treatment for nationals of other Contracting Parties is guaranteed.

The information supplied must cover guidance in both the education and labour market sectors.

Subsequent reports

Report any changes in the guidance services (eg. new possibilities, increase in the percentage of GDP devoted to guidance, new statistics, etc.). Supply texts of any new laws on vocational guidance.

Article 10 – The right to vocational training

The right to vocational training guaranteed by Article 10 is a prerequisite for enjoyment of the other Charter rights, particularly the right to work (Article 1). This connection between vocational training and the right to work is spelt out in Article 1 para. 4, which requires Contracting Parties to "provide or promote appropriate vocational guidance, training and rehabilitation".

As regards the scope of Article 10:

i. Self-employed people are covered in some relevant cases (Article 10 para. 3 is one example).

ii. Foreigners are covered if they are nationals of other Contracting Parties, legally resident or working in the state concerned. Equal treatment for foreigners must exist not only in law, but also in practice, and must apply to all aspects of Article 10.

iii. The Committee looks at vocational training for people with disabilities under Article 15, for states which have accepted both provisions.

Under Article 33, Contracting Parties fulfil their commitments if at least 80% of the people concerned enjoy the rights guaranteed by Article 10.

Paragraph 1 – Technical and vocational training – Access to higher technical and university education

This provision obliges Contracting Parties to do two things:

a. To promote technical and vocational training for all

The Committee examines the state's general vocational training policy and the overall structure of the training system which follows compulsory schooling, including the role of management and labour in planning and implementing training. It takes a special interest in basic vocational training in schools, where it is not part of an apprenticeship scheme, this being covered by paragraph 2 (see below).

The main indicators of compliance include total spending on vocational training, the system's total capacity (in particular, whether there are as many training places as there are candidates), the percentage of young people who complete vocational training courses, and geographical coverage.

b. *To provide access to higher technical and university education with individual aptitude as sole criterion*

Paragraph 2 – Apprenticeship and other training schemes for young people

Paragraph 2 concerns apprenticeship and "other systematic arrangements for training young boys and girls in their various employments". These types of training must combine theoretical and practical training, and close ties must be maintained between training establishments and the working world.

The indicators of compliance with this paragraph are the number of people in training, the availability of apprenticeships for all those seeking them, the percentage of young people who complete apprenticeship training, and geographical coverage.

Paragraph 3 – Vocational training and retraining of adult workers

Paragraph 3 obliges states to provide or promote vocational training for adults.

The indicators of compliance with this provision are: the types of adult training and education available on the labour market (particularly vocational training and retraining for the unemployed), training measures for certain groups, such as women, the number of persons in training, trends in state spending and the impact of the efforts made, eg. on employment.

Paragraph 4 – Measures to encourage full use of training facilities

This provision obliges states to do four specific things both for nationals and for foreigners protected by the Charter:

– to reduce or abolish any fees or charges;

– to grant financial aid in appropriate cases;

– to include in normal working hours time spent on extra training at an employer's request;

– to monitor the effectiveness of apprenticeship and other training schemes for young people in consultation with employers' and workers' organisations.

Information which national reports must include

First report

Answer all the questions on the Form for Reports, and give details of the vocational training system's structure, its workings (including geographical coverage and the parts played by the public and private sectors), the measures taken and the role of management and labour in planning and implementing vocational training policy.

Provide all the relevant figures, including total expenditure, number of training centres, number of participants, number of diplomas awarded and availability of training places, and provide an assessment of the results achieved. Also supply information enabling the Committee to determine whether nationals of other Contracting Parties are given equal treatment.

Subsequent reports

Report any changes in law or practice during the reference period and supply the latest figures.

Article 11 – The right to protection of health

The Social Charter contains a number of provisions which call, explicitly or implicitly, for health protection. The rights guaranteed by Article 2 (the right to just conditions of work) are based on the need to protect people's health at work. Article 3 lays down obligations concerning health and safety at work. Articles 7 and 17 protect the health and safety of children and young people. Articles 8 and 17 protect the health of pregnant women, and Articles 12 and 13 cover social security and medical assistance. Health is also important in connection with the rights of migrant workers, and particularly family reunion. Alongside these various provisions, Article 11 covers public health in the broad sense: removing the causes of ill-health, promoting health education and a sense of personal responsibility in health matters, and preventing disease.

The Committee's case law on Article 11 covers numerous issues which affect public health, eg. food safety, environmental protection, vaccination programmes and alcohol abuse.

Paragraph 1 – Removing the causes of ill-health

The Committee of Social Rights makes a global assessment of compliance with this provision, *inter alia* by examining:

- the measures taken by states to provide proper medical and paramedical care. It pays special attention to vulnerable groups and to perinatal and infant health. If indicators (eg. infant mortality figures) are clearly unreasonable, it concludes that the state concerned is not complying;
- environmental protection measures and steps taken to ensure food safety and reduce air, soil, water and noise pollution;
- how various diseases are treated: AIDS, mental disorders, diseases related to smoking, drinking, drug abuse, etc;
- information on staffing levels in the health services, the number of establishments (hospitals, dispensaries, medical centres, etc.), and their location.

Paragraph 2 – Advisory and education facilities

This provision requires Contracting Parties to provide advisory and education facilities in the health field.

Here again, the Committee makes a global assessment of national compliance with the Charter, making sure that sufficient resources and technical skills are deployed for this activity.

Health care for pregnant women and elderly persons is also important in the case law. The Committee looks at the range of services provided for all these groups and their accessibility in terms of cost and location.

The provision of health education in schools is one key aspect of compliance with this provision.

The Committee looks at information on all other activities, eg. campaigns to make the public aware of the need to guard against disease and live healthily: media used, target groups and success rate. Questions to which it attaches special importance include AIDS, smoking, drinking and nutrition.

Paragraph 3 – Disease prevention

This provision obliges states to take action to prevent epidemic and endemic diseases. Here again, the Committee makes a global assessment, focusing on the following factors:

a. *Vaccination practice*

The Committee ascertains whether vaccinations are compulsory and whether they are provided free of charge. Parties must show that their vaccination programmes are widely accessible and cover a majority of the population. The Committee also compares their vaccination rates with the targets set by the World Health Organisation.

b. *Measures concerning infectious diseases*

The Committee analyses all the data available on national situations, to see how well governments cope with infectious diseases: arrangements for reporting diseases, isolation of people suffering from serious infectious diseases, special treatment for AIDS patients, etc. One of the other factors considered is the prevention of nosocomial infections (ie. those contracted during hospital treatment).

Information which national reports must include

First report

Answer all the questions on the Form for Reports and describe the public health system, indicating the extent and range of health problems in the population and the measures taken to prevent and cure them.

Subsequent reports

Report any changes during the reference period and supply the latest figures.

Article 12 – The right to social security

The distinction between social security and social assistance is highly controversial, but appears in the Social Charter, where social security and social assistance are dealt with in two different Articles (12 and 13), establishing different obligations. It must therefore be taken into account.

"Social assistance" applies to benefits granted essentially on the basis of individual need, without the recipient's having to belong to a social security scheme covering a specific risk, to be actively employed or to pay contributions. The beneficiaries are persons who receive no social security benefits guaranteeing them an adequate income, or who cannot afford the medical treatment they need.

"Social security", covering both general schemes and occupational schemes, pays contributory, non-contributory or combined benefits in certain contingencies (sickness, incapacity for work, maternity, family charges, unemployment, old age, death, widowhood, occupational accidents and diseases). Benefits for certain contingencies are means-tested.

Although it takes account of states' views, the Committee of Social Rights ultimately decides for Charter purposes which benefits belong to social assistance, and which to social security.

Paragraph 1 – Establishing or maintaining a social security system

A social security system qualifies as such under paragraph 1 when:

– it covers certain major contingencies in a number of fields specified in ILO Convention No. 102 and provides the corresponding benefits;

– it covers a large proportion of the population.

Paragraph 2 – Maintaining a social security system at a satisfactory level at least equal to that required for ratification of International Labour Convention No. 102

States ratifying ILO Convention No. 102 undertake to provide at least three of the main branches of social security, to provide a minimum level of benefits, and to cover a certain percentage of a reference population, which may, at their own discretion, be wage-earners, the active population or the resident population. In addition, at least one of the following three branches must be accepted: unemployment, old age, occupational accidents, invalidity or survivors' benefits.

Article 12 para. 2 obliges Parties to accept three of the nine parts of ILO Convention No. 102.

The Committee bases its assessment on the findings of the ILO Committee of Experts concerning application of Convention No. 102.

It also considers the extent to which Parties apply the European Code of Social Security,[1] application of which is also monitored by the ILO Committee of Experts.

Parties are not necessarily obliged to ratify ILO Convention No. 102 before accepting Article 12 para. 2 of the Charter. In such cases, the Committee may base its assessment on their ratification of other ILO conventions which guarantee standards of protection higher than the minimum required by Convention No. 102. It may also decide for itself whether a given country complies with Convention No. 102.

Paragraph 3 – Progressive improvement of the social security system

This provision requires Parties to make an ongoing effort to raise the level of their social security systems progressively.

Whether or not they accept paragraph 2, Parties must provide at least the minimum level of protection required by Convention No. 102: improvements satisfy paragraph 3 only if the social security system in question was already up to the minimum standard required by the convention.

The Committee considered, for example, that one Party had shown its determination to improve its social security system by ratifying the European Code of Social Security.

---

1. The European Code of Social Security and ILO Convention No. 102 contain similar provisions, but states ratifying the Convention must accept at least three of its nine parts, while those ratifying the Code must accept at least six out of nine; the nine parts concern: medical care (II), sickness benefit (III), unemployment benefit (IV), old-age benefit (V), employment injury benefit (VI), family benefit (VII), maternity benefit (VIII), invalidity benefit (IX) and survivors' benefit (X).

However, an increase in benefits which simply covers the increase in the cost of living does not constitute an improvement.

The Committee has expressly accepted that a state may modify its social security system, provided that the changes are necessary to maintain it, and that any restrictions do not undermine the protection of all members of the community against social and economic risks, or generally tend to turn the social security system into a simple means of providing minimum assistance.

Since the economy and social rights are closely connected, the Committee considers that the pursuit of economic objectives is not necessarily incompatible with the obligation under Article 12 para. 3. Parties may consider that action to put public finances on a sounder footing (to avoid increasing deficits and debt servicing costs) can help to maintain the social security system, and specifically that action to reduce the cost of health care is consistent with that aim.

In deciding whether changes in social security systems are compatible with paragraph 3, the Committee considers the following factors:

– the nature of the changes made (scope, conditions of access, amount and duration of benefits, etc.);

– the reasons for the changes, and their social and economic context;

– the scope of the changes (groups and number of people concerned, amount of benefits before and after the changes);

– whether the changes are necessary and match both the situation which generated them and the aims pursued;

– the existence of assistance measures for persons left in need by the changes (this information may be submitted under Article 13 of the Charter);

– the results achieved by the changes.

There is one restriction, however: the goal of effective social protection for all members of society, which Parties accepting Article 12 para. 3 must pursue, requires them to maintain social security systems based on solidarity – which provides a fundamental guarantee against discrimination in this area. The collective nature of social security funding, based on contributions and/or taxes, is a key aspect of this guarantee, since it makes it possible to spread the cost of the contingencies covered over all the members of the group.

Paragraph 4 – Equal treatment for nationals of the other Contracting Parties with respect to social security

Under Article 12 para. 4, Contracting Parties undertake:

a. *To ensure equal treatment for their own nationals and nationals of other Contracting Parties.*

States may not restrict social benefits to their own nationals, or impose additional or restrictive conditions on foreigners only – apart from a prescribed period of residence, which is permitted in principle by the Appendix to the Charter. The Committee verifies, however, that the length of any such period is reasonable. Here, it should be noted that requirements which in theory apply equally to nationals and foreigners (particularly those concerning resident status and periods of residence) may in practice apply exclusively or essentially to foreigners, and so amount to indirect discrimination.

b. To permit the maintenance of social security rights.

This principle applies to long-term benefits (pensions), but may be restricted in the case of short-term benefits (eg. unemployment benefits).

c. To make it possible for migrants to maintain or recover their social security rights, in cases where these are subject to qualifying periods – for example by the accumulation of all previous periods of contribution or employment for that purpose.

These rights are secured by multilateral or bilateral agreements, or by unilateral measures.

Information which national reports must include

First report

Answer all the questions on the Form for Reports, and provide information on the social security systems (branches, how they are funded, number of people covered, *modus operandi*).

Send copies of the reports on application of ILO Convention No. 102 and other ILO conventions on social security, as well as copies of reports on application of the European Code of Social Security.

List all multilateral or bilateral agreements concluded with other Contracting Parties or, if there are no agreements, explain how equal treatment (see paragraph 4*a*, *b* and *c* above) is guaranteed.

Subsequent reports

Report any changes in law and practice during the reference period. Give details (see paragraph 3 above) of any restrictions or changes in the social security system.

Article 13 – The right to social and medical assistance

For an explanation of the distinction made in the Charter between social security and social assistance, see the introductory comments on Fact Sheet C – 12, concerning Article 12.

Paragraph 1 – The right of persons in need to adequate social and medical assistance

Under this provision, all nationals – and also foreigners covered by the Appendix to the Charter (see below) – who are without adequate resources have a personal right to appropriate social and medical assistance.

For the purposes of this provision, social assistance covers cash benefits and benefits in kind, including those restricted to certain beneficiaries and those available to everyone. Medical assistance covers free or subsidised health care, or payments enabling people to pay for the care they require.

Since this is a right, it must be enforceable. It must be clearly defined in law and based on objective criteria. It may not be subject to any condition of budgetary feasibility.

Persons applying for social assistance must be able to appeal if this is refused by the authorities. The appeal body must be independent and have power to examine the merits of the contested decision. If it is a non-judicial body, certain institutional features (eg. how members are appointed and for how long, their legal expertise, etc.) must guarantee its independence. To ensure that applicants effectively enjoy the right of appeal, legal aid must be available.

The level of assistance provided must not be manifestly disproportionate to the cost of living and/or the minimum subsistence level in the country concerned. The Committee makes a global assessment of the situation, looking at all the forms of assistance available (benefits in cash or kind, special allowances for underprivileged groups, etc.).

Since need is the only criterion referred to in Article 13 para. 1, any restrictive conditions are likely to violate the Charter. This means that a lower age limit (eg. twenty-five) is not compatible with the Charter, and the same applies to any restriction on the duration of assistance. The right to social assistance must be maintained for as long as the state of need persists. However, linking social assistance with willingness to look for work or undergo vocational training is compatible with the Charter, provided that these conditions are reasonable and in keeping with the aim pursued, namely to find a lasting solution to the person's problems (see paragraph 3 below). The right to appeal must again be guaranteed.

Under the Appendix to the Charter, all nationals of Contracting Parties lawfully resident or working in another Party's territory are entitled to social and medical assistance on the same conditions as that state's nationals. Conditions concerning length of residence or ordinary residence are not compatible with this provision, since they inevitably exclude certain people who need social assistance for a certain period. Such restrictions are likely to affect foreigners more than others, and so may be a source of indirect discrimination.

As long as their residence or work permits remain valid, nationals of Contracting Parties legally resident or working in another Party's territory may not be expelled solely because they are in need.

Paragraph 2 – No diminution of the political or social rights of persons in receipt of social or medical assistance

This provision obliges Parties to ensure that no domestic law deprives people of their social or political rights because they are receiving social or medical assistance. The Committee has noted several instances of non-compliance, eg. restrictions barring persons in receipt of social assistance from access to the public service. It has also ruled that requiring applicants for social assistance to have a fixed address may, in extreme cases, have the effect of depriving them of their right to social protection.

Nationals of Contracting Parties lawfully resident or working in another Party's territory are also covered by this provision, subject to the restrictions normally applying in Council of Europe member states to the political rights of foreign nationals.

Paragraph 3 – Services to help prevent, remove or alleviate personal or family want

The services referred to in this provision are the essential counterpart of the social and medical assistance provided for in Article 13 para. 1. Together, these provisions are designed to ensure that people are fully informed of their rights, and also to enable them to overcome their difficulties and support themselves instead of becoming dependent on benefits.

The national services concerned must be able to cater for this need. The Committee bases its assessment on a number of criteria:

– the services concerned, their composition, geographical location and field of action;

– staff (including volunteers), qualifications and duties;

– funding of these services;

– methods used to assess their powers.

These services must cover the entire country, and must be equally accessible to nationals of other Contracting Parties legally residing or working there.

Paragraph 4 – The right of nationals of Contracting Parties legally present, but not resident, in another Party's territory to social and medical assistance

This provision applies to nationals of the other Contracting Parties who are lawfully present in a Party's territory, but do not reside lawfully or work regularly there. Since their presence is temporary, appropriate forms of social and medical assistance do not necessarily include all the benefits available under the general scheme. Temporary assistance in an emergency is sufficient (food, accommodation, clothing, emergency medical care). In such cases, assistance must be given, regardless of local or national resources.

Persons covered by this provision may be repatriated, but the relevant provisions of the 1953 European Convention on Social and Medical Assistance must be respected.

Information which national reports must include

First report

Answer all the questions on the Form for Reports and list all forms of social assistance, including special assistance restricted to certain groups or situations. Give information on the number of people in permanent receipt of social assistance in each reference period and state the global assistance budget.

Send copies of the relevant laws, indicating the nature and scope of the rights concerned, and provide full explanations of any restrictions or conditions applied.

Explain the methods used to determine benefit levels and how they compare with other indicators, such as minimum wage, average wage and minimum social security benefit.

Show that the Charter's requirements concerning appeal are respected, supplying the relevant laws and, when appropriate, details of the appeal body's case law.

Subsequent reports

Report any changes in law and practice during the reference period, any change in the number of beneficiaries of social and medical assistance, the indexing of benefits, the total cost of social and medical assistance and its percentage share of the overall social protection budget.

Article 14 – The right to benefit from social welfare services

Paragraph 1 – The obligation to provide social welfare services

In accepting Article 14 para. 1 of the Charter, Contracting Parties undertake to set up a network of social services to help people to overcome any problems of social adjustment, whatever the causes or effects of those problems may be – personal, family-related, occupational, physical or psychological.

This commitment covers:

a. The provision of social welfare services for all groups likely to need them

Social welfare services within the meaning of Article 14 may focus on specific groups or be general. What counts is that groups which are naturally vulnerable – children, the elderly, people with disabilities, young people with problems and delinquents, minorities (migrants, gypsies, refugees, etc.), the homeless, alcohol and drug abusers, battered women and former prisoners – should be able to avail themselves of them in practice.

b. Effective access to social welfare services

The Committee makes sure that the right to these services is guaranteed in practice by verifying that:

– people wishing to use them may do so as of right and can appeal against unfair refusals;

– any financial contributions required are geared to the applicant's income;

– geographical distribution of these services is sufficiently wide;

– recourse to these services does not interfere with people's private lives;

– these services are open, without discrimination, to nationals of other Contracting Parties lawfully residing or regularly working in the state concerned.

c. Effectiveness of social welfare services

Services must have resources matching their responsibilities and the changing needs of users, ie.:

– human resources: qualified staff in sufficient numbers;

– institutional resources: decision-making centres as close to users as possible (decentralisation and delegation of responsibilities to local authorities);

– financial resources allowing them to do their job properly and pursue dynamic policies.

Paragraph 2 – Encouraging individuals and organisations to play a part in establishing and maintaining social welfare services

In accepting Article 14 para. 2, Contracting Parties agree:

a. To provide support for voluntary associations seeking to "establish" social welfare services

Article 14 imposes no set model, and states may achieve this goal in different ways: they may promote the establishment of social services jointly run by public bodies, private concerns and voluntary associations, or may leave the provision of certain services entirely to the voluntary sector.

The "individuals and voluntary or other organisations" referred to in paragraph 2 include the voluntary sector, private individuals, trade unions, employers' organisations, private firms, etc.

The Committee looks at all forms of support, financial (grants or tax incentives) and non-financial. It also verifies that the Parties are continuing to ensure that services are accessible to all and are effective, in keeping with the above criteria. Specifically, Parties must ensure that public and private services are properly co-ordinated, and that efficiency does not suffer because of the number of providers involved.

b. To encourage individuals and organisations to play a part in "maintaining" services

The Committee looks at action taken to strengthen dialogue with civil society in areas of welfare policy which affect the social welfare services. This includes action to promote representation of specific user-groups in bodies where the public authorities are also represented, and action to promote consultation of users on questions concerning organisation of the various social services and the aid they provide.

Information which national reports must include

First report

Answer all the questions on the Form for Reports and describe the main social welfare services: tasks, users, conditions of access, geographical distribution, organisation and working methods, funding and links with social security institutions, staff numbers and qualifications, arrangements for appeal.

Also report any measures taken to support private initiative in the establishment and maintenance of social welfare services, and to foster co-ordination between the various parties involved.

Subsequent reports

Report any changes in law or practice during each reference period and indicate any progress made in furthering the development of the social welfare services. State what steps have been taken to maintain effective services, with resources matching their responsibilities and the changing needs of users.

Article 15 – The right of people with disabilities to vocational training, rehabilitation and social resettlement

The aim of Article 15 is to guarantee equal employment opportunities for people with disabilities. Contracting Parties undertake to introduce special vocational training (paragraph 1) and employment (paragraph 2) measures for people with disabilities, with a view to improving their chances of finding work. Article 15 is one of the three Charter provisions which apply the general principle laid down in Article 1 para. 4 in detailed practice.[1] It differs from the other two – Articles 9 (right to vocational guidance) and 10 (right to vocational training) – in imposing more extensive obligations on Parties, including that of taking positive action.

Article 15 applies to people with physical and/or mental disabilities.

Paragraph 1 – The right of people with disabilities to vocational training

Vocational training for people with disabilities is treated as a continuous process, covering basic training at school, technical training leading to formal qualifications, and retraining for people with disabilities caused by occupational accidents or diseases.

A necessary concomitant of this process is regular appraisal of the occupational aptitudes of people with disabilities, the aim being – with their agreement – to devise a rehabilitation programme to match their needs and abilities.

The effort to provide training must not stop at formulation of a programme: Article 15 requires that suitable and sufficient training facilities be made available in practice. This means:

---

1. For the links between Article 15 and Article 1 para. 4, see the latter (Fact Sheet C – 1).

- providing the facilities which people with disabilities need to follow training programmes in normal conditions (teaching materials, access to premises, etc.);

- training instructors: all staff involved in the vocational rehabilitation of people with disabilities or, at an earlier stage, in assessment of their occupational aptitudes must receive proper training;

- providing financial aid to cover the extra costs of disability.

Paragraph 2 – The right of people with disabilities to employment

Article 15 does not require Parties to apply a specific policy for the placement and employment of people with disabilities. Provided they respect certain requirements concerning the aim of effective participation in economic life on an equal footing, they are free to choose whatever means they wish.

Article 15 para. 2 does not require them to set up special placement services for people with disabilities. The normal employment services may be used, provided that there are enough of them, and that they succeed in integrating people with disabilities into the ordinary working world. When both specialised and general services exist, Article 15 requires them to co-operate.

Under Article 15 para. 2, employment policy for people with disabilities must not stop at access to employment, but must also set out to integrate them permanently, eg. through measures to keep them in employment. For this purpose, employers must be subjected to obligations, both positive (rehabilitation) and negative (no employee must be dismissed because of disability).

Sheltered employment is a fall-back measure, for use only when placement in an ordinary working environment proves impossible, and should aim at eventual transfer to an ordinary post. People working in sheltered establishments, where production is the main activity, must enjoy the usual benefits of labour law, and particularly remuneration in keeping with the work done.

Information which national reports must include

First report

When answering the questions on the Form for Reports, indicate:

- the criteria your country's law uses to define people with disabilities;

- the number of people with disabilities, and the number of these who are of working age;

- the practical arrangements for assessing the occupational aptitudes of people with disabilities, and the extent to which they participate

in drawing up their vocational training and/or rehabilitation programmes;

- the number of applications for admission to the various types of
  vocational training and the number of places available (see, in particular, question F on the form);
- the percentage of the overall vocational training and employment
  budget devoted to training and employment for people with disabilities;
- if there is a quota for the employment of people with disabilities,
  the sectors to which it applies and the results obtained in terms of
  permanent employment for persons with disabilities;
- the measures taken to protect people with disabilities from dismissal.

The reports submitted under ILO Convention No. 159 (Vocational
Rehabilitation and Employment (Disabled Persons) 1983) should also
be supplied.

Subsequent reports

Report any changes in law or practice during the reference period for
each of the areas covered in the first two reports.

Article 16 – The right of the family to social, legal and economic protection

The family as "fundamental unit of society", is specifically protected by the Social Charter. The right of families to social, legal and economic protection under Article 16 obliges Contracting Parties to implement a genuine family policy by various means.

This Article covers a very broad area, extending well beyond the strictly civil aspects of family law to certain aspects of social and tax law (ie. family policy).

1. Equality of family rights

"Family" can mean different things in different places and at different times – so the Charter refers to the definitions used in national law. The Committee has never made distinctions between the various models of family, apart from providing greater protection for certain more vulnerable types, eg. single-parent families.

2. Equality of spouses' and children's rights

The Charter insists that spouses must be equal, particularly in respect of rights and duties within the couple (marital authority, ownership, administration and use of property, etc.) and children (establishment of parentage, adoption, parental authority, management of children's property).

Article 16 implies that Contracting Parties must provide for various forms of family mediation to settle disputes and protect families. When families break up, the protection guaranteed by Article 16 applies in particular to children. States must therefore take account of children's interests when settling questions of custody and access, and allow them to express their views in proceedings concerning them.

3. Family policy and protection of the social bond

Article 16 gives a non-exhaustive list of family policy instruments. Subject to certain minimum requirements, Parties are free to choose their own means of achieving the following results:

a. Guarantee of an adequate standard of living for families

Article 16 requires Contracting Parties to operate a family benefits scheme. The obligations it imposes in respect of family benefits are thus more specific than those under Article 12 (see Fact Sheet C – 12). Benefits must cover a significant number of families and be sufficient to provide them with an adequate income supplement. They must be regularly reviewed to keep pace with inflation.

As with Article 12 para. 4, nationals of other Contracting Parties must enjoy equal treatment concerning all aspects of Article 16. Since family benefits are generally non-contributory, entitlement may be subject to a qualifying period of residence, provided that this period:

– concerns only the parents of the children for whom benefit is paid, and not the children themselves;

– is not unduly long;

– does not apply solely, or proportionally more, to foreigners.

Like family benefits, tax concessions for families with children can help to maintain their standard of living. The Committee has not made such arrangements a compulsory requirement under Article 16, but regards them as fully in keeping with the spirit of that provision.

Contracting Parties are also required to adopt special measures for single-parent and low-income families.

b. The construction of suitable family housing

Article 16 requires Parties to help fund the building of family housing and to have a sufficient supply of subsidised housing.

They must also provide financial aid to help families accede to housing.

Finally, they must ensure that their housing policies meet the needs of families (housing units which are sufficiently large, and have the essential facilities).

c. Suitable child-care arrangements for families

Child-minding services, particularly for infants, must exist in sufficient numbers to meet families' needs, must offer a high standard of service and must be accessible to all.

Information which national reports must include

First report

Answer all the questions on the Form for Reports.

Information should also be supplied on the following:

– Family benefits:

Parties which have not ratified the European Code of Social Security must supply information on:

- categories of person protected (ie. specified groups of workers (a) or specified groups of the active population (b)). In case (a), the number of workers protected under the general scheme and/or special schemes and the total number of workers. In case (b), the number of active persons protected under the general scheme and/or special schemes and the total number of residents;

- the size of the regular allowances for each dependent child;

- the total number of children of all residents;

- the total value of cash benefits paid for the children of protected persons;

- the wage of an unskilled male worker (standard beneficiary).

– Child care services:

- the number of children from 0 to 3 years old;

- the number and capacity of public child-minding facilities;

- their geographical distribution;

- supervision of the quality of the services provided (eg. existence of approval procedures);

- fees policy for public child-minding services (cost coverage and percentage paid by parents) and any subsidies for private services;

- housing: national housing budget, data on the construction of family housing, occupation rate, proportion of family budget spent on rent.

Subsequent reports

Report any changes in family law and family policy and update figures asked for in previous reports.

Article 17 – The right of mothers and children to social and economic protection

Article 17 supplements the rights given children by Article 7, and families by Article 16. In particular, it covers:

– the protection of mothers;

– the status of children;

– the protection of young people in general.

1. The protection of mothers[1]

The Charter only refers to measures in favour of mothers. These measures include institutions and services to protect children and mothers and to provide mothers who have no social security coverage with financial aid before and after childbirth, and with medical assistance or the services of a midwife when giving birth.

There must there be no discrimination against single mothers, and Parties must also take special measures for them, for example by providing guidance and assistance, including financial assistance.

2. The status of children

Article 17 applies mainly to children below school age. However, in so far as it applies to the legal status of children born out of wedlock, it may also cover adults.

The main obligations under Article 17 concerning the status of children are:

---

1. The protection provided by Article 17 does not cover single fathers, who are, however, covered by Article 16. Article 16 of the revised Charter contains measures for single parents.

a. *The establishment of parentage*

This concerns research to establish paternity or maternity, and also adoption. The Committee's main interest in procedures to establish natural parentage concerns categories of children unable to use those procedures.

b. *The rights of children born out of wedlock*

Article 17 of the Charter permits no discrimination between children born out of wedlock, and children born in wedlock, eg. in respect of maintenance obligations and inheritance rights.

c. *The protection of orphans and homeless children*

Article 17 obliges Parties to provide homeless children with the nearest possible approximation to a normal home environment. They are thus required to provide such children with special care and protection, to ensure that their development and well-being are not too seriously impaired.

The same applies to orphans, who must also be given legal guarantees concerning custody or guardianship and the administration of their property.

3. The protection of young people in general

Article 17 requires Contracting Parties to take measures in the following fields:

– protection of children against ill-treatment;

– access for children to civil and criminal courts;

– protection of young offenders (age of criminal responsibility; age at which sanctions can be imposed; sanctions applied and forms of enforcement; types of education and care provided).

Information which national reports must include

First report

Answer all the questions on the Form for Reports. Enclose the corresponding laws.

Supply information on the state of the law and its application in all areas regarded as particularly important by the Committee, ie. the protection of children against ill-treatment, access for children to civil and criminal courts, and the protection of young offenders.

Concerning protection against ill-treatment (including sexual abuse), give information on the extent of the problem and on measures – preventive or otherwise – taken or envisaged to give children and young people the protection to which they are entitled, also within families.

Add information on any services (including social and legal services) set up for this purpose, on their responsibilities and on the regulations which govern their work.

Concerning access to civil and criminal courts, state whether provision is made for children to be represented before the courts and, if so, describe the arrangements, particularly in cases of dispute with or between parents, guardians or administrators. State also whether children themselves may be heard by the courts and, if so, from what age and in what circumstances.

Regarding the protection of young offenders, in addition to the information asked for under G on the report form, provide information on the age of criminal responsibility, the age at which sanctions may be imposed, and what the sanctions are and how they are enforced, especially when they involve imprisonment. Finally, provide information on protection measures, and on education and care provided for and actually dispensed.

Subsequent reports

Update information given in the previous report and answer the Committee's specific questions.

Article 18 – The right to engage in a gainful occupation in the territory of other Contracting Parties

Article 18 of the Charter does not recognise the right, as such, to enter and remain in a Contracting Party's territory.

It concerns the pursuit of gainful occupations by nationals of other Parties lawfully in the territory concerned.

Paragraph 1 – Applying existing regulations in a liberal spirit

Paragraph 2 – Simplifying formalities and reducing dues and charges

Paragraph 3 – Liberalising regulations

The Committee assesses a country's overall compliance with these three provisions.

In accepting them, Contracting Parties undertake:

– not to limit, de jure or de facto, authorisation to engage in a gainful occupation to a specific post for a specific employer; however, economic or social reasons may justify restricting the employment of aliens to specific types of job in certain occupational and geographical sectors;

– to liberalise as far as possible the formalities required of persons wishing to obtain or renew authorisation to engage in or continue a gainful activity as employees or in their own employ; furthermore, the fees and dues payable to obtain such authorisation or renewal must not be too high.

Paragraph 4 – The right of nationals to leave the country

In accepting this provision, Contracting Parties undertake not to restrict the right of their own nationals to leave the country to pursue gainful activities in other contracting states.

The only restrictions allowed are those provided for in Article 31 of the Charter, ie. those which are "prescribed by law and are necessary in a democratic society for the protection of the rights and freedoms of others or for the protection of public interest, national security, public health or morals".

Information which national reports must include

First report

Provide the information asked for on the Form for Reports.

Subsequent reports

Report any changes in law or practice during the reference period.

Article 19 – The right of migrants and their families to protection and assistance

The purpose of Article 19 is to improve the legal, social and material situation of migrants and their families, in order to guarantee them the same treatment as nationals.

It applies to nationals of Contracting Parties lawfully residing or regularly working in the territory of other Parties.

When assessing compliance, the Committee of Social Rights takes account of migration flow patterns.

Paragraph 1 – Free information and assistance services; measures to counter misleading propaganda relating to emigration and immigration

The Contracting Parties undertake to provide free information and assistance services, and also to prevent misleading propaganda relating to emigration and immigration.

They must provide these services for home nationals wishing to emigrate to other Contracting States, and also for nationals of the other states wishing to enter their territory.

Paragraph 2 – Measures to facilitate the departure, journey and reception of migrant workers and their families

This paragraph requires states to adopt measures to facilitate the departure, journey and reception of migrants.

Reception must include help with placement and integration in the workplace, and also with certain other problems, such as short-term accommodation, illness or shortage of money. It must also include proper health measures.

Paragraph 3 – Co-operation between social services in emigration and immigration countries

These services include all those public and private organisations which help migrants and their families to cope with everyday problems, adjust to their new surroundings and also keep in touch with family members who have stayed behind in their own country. Appropriate co-operation must be established between social services, both public and private, in emigration and immigration countries, so that migrant families can be helped with any personal or family problems.

In the absence of systematic co-operation, arrangements for ad hoc co-operation must exist.

Paragraph 4 – Equal treatment for migrants in respect of employment conditions, trade union membership and accommodation

Contracting Parties are required to eliminate all legal or de facto discrimination concerning:

a. remuneration and other employment and working conditions, including in-service training and promotion;

b. trade union membership and enjoyment of the benefits of collective bargaining, including access to administrative and managerial posts in trade unions;

c. access to public, and also private housing. There must be no legal or de facto restrictions on home-buying, access to subsidised housing, or housing aids, such as loans or other allowances.

Paragraph 5 – Equal treatment of migrants with regard to employment taxes, dues or contributions

Under this paragraph, there must be fully equal treatment in all these fields, both in law and in practice.

Paragraph 6 – Family reunion

Paragraph 6 requires Parties to allow the families of foreign workers legally established in their territory to join them.

The family members concerned are the migrant's wife and dependent children under twenty-one years of age.

"Dependent" children are those who have no independent existence outside the family group, particularly for economic or health reasons, or because they are pursuing unpaid studies.

A state may not refuse entry into its territory for family reunion purposes on health grounds unless the illness is likely to endanger public health or public order.

This paragraph also sets the legal age limit for dependent children rejoining their families at twenty-one. Since the age limit in most Contracting Parties is eighteen, the Committee considers the actual situation, asking them to produce figures showing that children between the ages of eighteen and twenty-one are allowed to rejoin their families in practice.

Paragraph 7 – Equal treatment for migrants in respect of legal proceedings

States must ensure that migrants have access to courts, the assistance of lawyers and legal aid on the same conditions as their own nationals. This obligation applies to all legal proceedings concerning the rights guaranteed by Article 19.

Paragraph 8 – Protection against expulsion

This provision requires Contracting Parties to prohibit by law the expulsion of migrants lawfully working in their territory, except where they are a threat to national security or offend against public order or morality.

In addition under paragraph 8, foreign nationals served with expulsion orders must have right of appeal to a court or other independent body, even in cases where national security, public order or morality are at stake.

Paragraph 9 – Transfer of earnings and savings

This provision requires that Contracting Parties place no restrictions on the right of migrant workers to transfer earnings and savings, either during their stay or when they leave.

Migrants must be allowed to transfer money to their own country or any other country.

Paragraph 10 – Extension of protection and assistance provided to self-employed migrants

The protection and assistance provided for in paragraphs 1 to 9 must extend to self-employed migrants.

Contracting Parties must ensure that there is no discrimination, in law or in practice, either between salaried and self-employed migrants or between self-employed migrants and self-employed nationals.

Information which national reports must include

First report

Provide the information asked for on the Form for Reports.

Answer the general question asked in Conclusions XIV-1 (p. 45) concerning the eligibility of trade union delegates who are nationals of other Contracting Parties to sit on works councils and other official bodies on which labour and management are represented.

Subsequent reports

Report any changes during the reference period.

Article 1 of the 1988 Additional Protocol (Protocol No. 1) – The right to equal opportunities and equal treatment in matters of employment and occupation without discrimination on the grounds of sex

Contracting Parties undertake to recognise the right to equal opportunities and equal treatment in matters of employment and occupation without discrimination on grounds of sex, and to take appropriate action to ensure or promote equality in the following areas:

- access to employment, protection against dismissal and occupational resettlement;

- vocational guidance, training, retraining and rehabilitation;

- terms of employment and working conditions, including remuneration;

- career development, including promotion.

Acceptance of Article 1 obliges Parties to:

- embody the rights concerned in legislation;

- take legal measures to ensure their effectiveness;

- devise and implement active policies for that same purpose.

The rights and obligations embodied in Article 1 of the Protocol supplement the Charter provisions proper, particularly Articles 1 para. 2 and 4 para. 3. However, the material scope of Article 1 of the Protocol differs from that of those two Charter articles: whereas Article 1 para. 2 of the Charter covers discrimination on other grounds too, Article 1 of the Additional Protocol concerns gender discrimination only; and, whereas Article 4 para. 3 of the Charter specifically concerns equal pay for work of equal value, Article 1 of the Protocol – while also covering remuneration – is generally wider in its scope.

Article 1 of the Protocol also imposes broader obligations on Contracting Parties than Articles 1 para. 2 and 4 para. 3 of the Charter in their respective areas.

In the four areas specified in Article 1, states are required to give all salaried employees a legal right to take action before a court or other competent authority: the availability of judicial remedies is essential to effective enjoyment of the rights guaranteed by this provision.

Another essential requirement is that any clauses in collective agreements or employment contracts which contravene the principle of non-discrimination should be legally invalid in Contracting States. The courts must have authority to suspend application of any clause which violates the legal principle of equal treatment.

States must also take measures to deter employers from applying, even without knowing it, clauses which are likely to be declared invalid. Such measures might involve:

- legislating to make such clauses automatically invalid;

- allowing courts to declare them invalid *erga omnes;*

- giving trade unions an independent right to take legal action in these matters, including the right to appear as a party in individual disputes;

- allowing persons with an interest in having such clauses declared invalid to take collective action.

Legislation must also provide adequate safeguards against discriminatory and retaliatory measures. The law must provide for rectification of the situation complained of (reinstatement in cases of dismissal) and for compensation for any financial losses sustained in the interim. When this solution is impossible, financial compensation may be accepted instead, but only if it is sufficient to deter the employer and compensate the worker. The law may also provide for other sanctions for employers who practise discrimination.

The rule on burden of proof must also be partly reversed in cases of alleged gender discrimination. When a person claims that the equal treatment guaranteed by this provision has been denied and adduces, before a court or other competent authority, facts from which discrimination can be inferred, then the respondent must show that the apparent discrimination is due to objective factors, which have nothing to do with discrimination on grounds of sex, and so does not violate the equal treatment principle.

Article 1 para. 3 of the Additional Protocol explicitly provides for the adoption of measures to remove *de facto* inequalities. This means that states' domestic law may not exclude positive action in favour of one gender if the current situation makes this necessary.

Contracting Parties are also obliged to devise and implement active policies to ensure that the rights guaranteed by Article 1 are respected in practice.

As with other Charter provisions, Contracting Parties must take the action needed for appropriate, practical enforcement of their laws and regulations in this field. Although the Committee has not yet specified the conditions which Parties must fulfil in practice to satisfy this provision of the Protocol, it does ask for detailed information on the situation (see below). It will define the Parties' obligations clearly during the next supervision cycle covering this provision.

Information which national reports must include

First report

Answer the questions on the Form for Reports on the application of the 1988 Additional Protocol, and also the questions asked in the general observations in Conclusions XIII-5, pp. 254-257. Provide copies of the relevant laws.

Concerning the four areas covered by Article 1, supply detailed information on the situation in practice, ie.:

- the employment situation of men and women (numbers of men and women employed, unemployed, working part-time, working on fixed-term or insecure contracts);

- access to, and participation in, vocational training, retraining and rehabilitation, and particularly the extent to which women are trained for work traditionally done by men and vice-versa;

- any differences in employment conditions, including remuneration (indicating what differences exist between full-time employees on permanent contracts and part-time employees or those on fixed-term or other insecure contracts);

- differences between the sexes in terms of career development in the various sectors of the economy.

Also, to allow the Committee to assess the effectiveness of the active policies which Parties to the Protocol have introduced to achieve equality of opportunity and treatment in the employment field, indicate practical measures taken for this purpose.

Subsequent reports

Update the information provided in the previous report and answer the Committee's specific questions.

Article 2 of the 1988 Additional Protocol (Protocol No. 1) – The right to information and consultation on the economic and financial situation of the undertaking

Paragraph a requires Contracting Parties to provide workers or their representatives, regularly or whenever necessary, with information on the economic and financial situation of the firms which employ them.

The second obligation, set out in paragraph b, requires them to consult workers or their representatives in good time on proposed decisions which may substantially affect their interests, particularly on decisions which may have an important impact on the employment situation in the firm concerned.

These rights must be effectively guaranteed. In particular, workers must have legal remedies when they are not respected. There must also be sanctions for firms which fail to meet their obligations under this Article.

Information which national reports must include

First report

Answer all the questions on the Form for Reports on the application of the 1988 Additional Protocol.

Supply details of the legal remedies open to workers when their rights are not respected, and of the sanctions which may be imposed on firms failing to fulfil their obligations.

State whether nationals of other Contracting Parties lawfully residing or working in the country enjoy the rights guaranteed by Article 2 of the Additional Protocol.

Subsequent reports

Report any changes in law or practice during the reference period.

Article 3 of the 1988 Additional Protocol (Protocol No. 1) – The right to take part in the determination and improvement of the working conditions and working environment

Article 3 of the Additional Protocol requires Parties to organise the right of workers to participate in firms in the following areas:

– determining and improving working conditions, and organising work and the working environment (Article 3 para. 1*a*);

– protecting health and safety in the firm (Article 3 para. 1*b*);

– organising social and socio-cultural services and facilities in the firm (Article 3 para. 1*c*);

– monitoring compliance with the regulations on these matters (Article 3 para. 1*d*).

These rights must be effectively guaranteed. In particular, workers must have legal remedies when they are not respected. There must also be sanctions for firms which fail to meet their obligations under this Article.

Information which national reports must include

First report

Answer all the questions on the Form for Reports on the application of the 1988 Additional Protocol.

Supply details of the legal remedies open to workers when their rights are not respected, and of the sanctions which may be imposed on firms failing to fulfil their obligations.

State whether nationals of other Contracting Parties lawfully residing or working in the country enjoy the rights guaranteed by Article 3 of the Additional Protocol.

Subsequent reports

Report any changes in law or practice during the reference period.

Article 4 of the 1988 Additional Protocol (Protocol No. 1) – The right of elderly persons to social protection

Article 4 requires Parties to devise and implement coherent measures to ensure social protection for elderly people in the various areas covered by this provision. These measures must:

– enable elderly people to remain full members of the community for as long as possible (Article 4 para. 1);

– enable them to choose their life-style freely and lead independent lives in their accustomed surroundings for as long as they wish and are able to do so (Article 4 para. 2);

– guarantee elderly persons living in institutions appropriate support, while respecting their privacy, and a say in determining living conditions in the institution (Article 4 para. 3).

Information which national reports must include

First report

Answer the questions on the Form for Reports on the application of the 1988 Additional Protocol.

State whether nationals of the other Contracting Parties lawfully residing or working in the country enjoy the rights guaranteed by Article 4 of the Additional Protocol.

Subsequent reports

Report any changes in law or practice during the reference period.

Article 20 paragraph 5 – Labour inspection

Article 20 para. 5 of the European Social Charter and Article A para. 4 of the revised European Social Charter provide that:

"Each Contracting Party shall maintain a system of labour inspection appropriate to national conditions".

The case law of several Charter provisions refers to the Labour Inspectorate and how it should participate in the implementation of these provisions. Particular focus appears in:

– Article 1 para. 2: non-discrimination in employment;
– Articles 2 para. 1 and 4 para. 2: reasonable working hours and increased pay for overtime work(especially concerning supervision of flexible working time arrangements);
– Article 3 para. 2: supervision of the observance of health and safety regulations:
– Article 7: supervision of the observance of the prohibition of employment for children under the age of fifteen years and specific conditions for employment between fifteen and eighteen years of age;
– Article 8: prohibition of dismissal during maternity leave and certain special conditions for the employment of women;
– Article 15: vocational integration of persons with disabilities;
– Article 19: equal treatment for migrants.

The Labour Inspectorate should be invested with appropriate means in order to fulfil its duties:

– access to the workplace;
– possibility of taking immediate remedial action in cases of breach of regulations (Article 3 of the Charter);
– possibility of sanctions.

It is also important that services are sufficiently staffed by qualified personnel who regularly undergo further training.

The number of enterprises inspected, of workers covered by visits and of offences registered are also part of the criteria used by the Committee to assess the effective operation of labour inspection services.

Article 31 – Restrictions to the rights guaranteed by the Charter

Article 31 of the Charter is worded as follows:

"1 The rights and principles set forth in Part I when effectively realised, and their effective exercise as provided for in Part II, shall not be subject to any restrictions or limitations not specified in those parts, except such as are prescribed by law and are necessary in a democratic society for the protection of the rights and freedoms of others or for the protection of public interest, national security, public health, or morals.

2 The restrictions permitted under this Charter to the rights and obligations set forth herein shall not be applied for any purpose other than that for which they have been prescribed."

These provisions correspond to paragraphs 2 of Articles 8 to 11 of the European Convention on Human Rights, according to which:

"Article 8 para. 2

There shall be no interference by a public authority with the exercise of this right except such as is in accordance with the law and is necessary in a democratic society in the interests of national security, public safety or the economic well-being of the country, for the prevention of disorder or crime, for the protection of health or morals, or for the protection of the rights and freedoms of others.

(...)

Article 9 para. 2

Freedom to manifest one's religion or beliefs shall be subject only to such limitations as are prescribed by law and are necessary in a democratic society in the interests of public safety, for the protection of public order, health or morals, or for the protection of the rights and freedoms of others.

(...)

Article 10 para. 2

The exercise of these freedoms, since it carries with it duties and responsibilities, may be subject to such formalities, conditions, restrictions or penalties as are prescribed by law and are necessary in a democratic society, in the interests of national security, territorial integrity or public safety, for the prevention of disorder or crime, for the protection of health or morals, for the protection of the reputation or rights of others, for preventing the disclosure of information received in confidence, or for maintaining the authority and impartiality of the judiciary.

(...)

Article 11 para. 2

No restrictions shall be placed on the exercise of these rights other than such as are prescribed by law and are necessary in a democratic society in the interests of national security or public safety, for the prevention of disorder or crime, for the protection of health or morals or for the protection of the rights and freedoms of others. This article shall not prevent the imposition of lawful restrictions on the exercise of these rights by members of the armed forces, of the police or of the administration of the State."

Thus a restriction may only be put to one of the rights guaranteed by the Charter if it is:

1. it is provided for in the legislation;

2. necessary in a democratic society;

3. it is intended to achieve one of the following aims;

 - guarantee the respect of individual rights and liberties;

 - protect public order;

 - protect national security;

 - protect public health;

 - protect public morals.

The Committee has particularly devoted its attention under this Charter provision to restrictions of the right to bargain collectively (Article 6 para. 2) and to take collective action (Article 6 para. 4), especially in relation to interference with the right to strike.[1]

The Committee also refers to Article 31 under other provisions:

– Article 1 para. 2 (prohibition of forced labour): requisitioning of ships' crews is only justified if the safety of the ship or of those on board is at risk;

---

1. See for example: the use of arbitration to put a stop to collective action without the authorisation of the parties can only be justified if the situation at hand is covered by the scope of Article 31. The definition of the minimum services which should be maintained in the case of a strike must be restricted to the cases designated by that article.

– Article 19 para. 6 (family reunion): health grounds do not justify refusal of family reunion unless an illness represents a danger to public health or public order;
– Article 19 para. 8 (guarantee against expulsion): expulsion of migrant workers on grounds of ill-health is not justified except where, following a refusal of treatment for instance, the person concerned is a danger to public order.

Article 33 – Application of certain provisions of the Charter to the great majority of the workers concerned (80% rule)

Article 33 para. 1 of the Charter provides that Parties will be regarded as satisfying certain Charter provisions if they apply them to "a great majority of workers". The Committee considers that this means at least 80% of the workers concerned.

According to the rule, the provisions concerned may be implemented either by law or by collective agreements or any other means.

The provisions to which this rule applies are:
- Article 2 para. 1
- Article 2 para. 2
- Article 2 para. 3
- Article 2 para. 4
- Article 2 para. 5
- Article 7 para. 4
- Article 7 para. 6
- Article 7 para. 7
- Article 7 para. 8 (because of the Appendix to the Charter)
- Article 10 para. 1
- Article 10 para. 2
- Article 10 para. 3
- Article 10 para. 4
- Article 2 of Protocol No. 1
- Article 3 of Protocol No. 1

In practice, Contracting Parties must provide the Committee with all the information it needs to verify that the 80% rule is respected.

Any law which is inherently incompatible with a Charter provision, and potentially applies to all workers, is – even if it affects fewer than 20% of workers in practice – unacceptable under the Charter. One example, under Article 2 para. 1, is certain laws on working hours.

In cases where rights guaranteed by one of the above provisions are implemented through collective agreements, Parties must indicate which categories of worker are covered, and which are not, so that the Committee can verify that the 80% rule is respected.

Part D
Quiz – Fifty questions on the Social Charter

Questions

1. Is ratification of the Charter obligatory for Council of Europe member states? Or for new member states?

2. What are the core provisions:
   - of the Charter?
   - of the revised Charter?

3. What is the minimum number of provisions countries are required to accept:
   - in the Charter (...Articles or ...paragraphs)?
   - in the revised Charter (...Articles or ...paragraphs)?

4. How many countries have accepted all the Charter's provisions? Which?

5. How often do governments submit reports?

6. How many members does the European Committee of Social Rights have?

7. What is the composition of the Governmental Committee?

8. How do the social partners (employers' associations and trade unions) participate in the supervisory machinery?

9. Which supervisory machinery documents are public and when do they become so?

10. What is a warning?
    - who addresses it?
    - in what circumstances?
    - what is its legal status?

11. What is a recommendation?
    - who adopts it?
    - since when?
    - what majority is required?

12. How many recommendations has the Committee of Ministers adopted?

13. What is the Parliamentary Assembly's role in the supervisory procedure?

14. What forms of discrimination are prohibited by the Charter?

15. In what circumstances does the Charter's case law draw on the notion of indirect discrimination?

16. What rights are recognised by both the Charter and the European Convention on Human Rights?

17. What rights recognised by the United Nations Covenant on Economic, Social and Cultural Rights are not recognised by the Charter or the revised Charter?

18. What are the cultural rights recognised by the Charter?

19. What rights are included in the Additional Protocol of 1988?

20. What are the amended provisions in the revised Charter?

21. What are the new rights in the revised Charter?

22. Who can lodge collective complaints?

23. What is the Governmental Committee's role in the collective complaints procedure?

24. What is the Committee of Ministers' role in the collective complaints procedure?

25. What are the admissibility conditions for collective complaints?

26. According to the European Committee of Social Rights, what rights have to be enshrined in law to be effective?

27. What provisions of the Charter are deemed to be respected if the rules that implement them apply to at least 80% of the population concerned?

28. What persons are protected by the Charter (its scope *ratione personae*)?

29. To what extent are foreigners eligible for social assistance?

30. What provisions of the Charter entail a right of appeal to the domestic courts?

31. How does the European Committee of Social Rights monitor Article 1 para. 1 of the Charter: "right to work – full employment"?

32. How many public holidays does the Charter require?

33. What are the conditions for a country to be in compliance with Article 4 para. 3, which requires equal pay for women and men for work of equal value?

34. What is meant by work of equal value, as provided for in Article 4 para. 3 of the Charter?

35. What according to the Charter is the "decency threshold" for remuneration?

36. How are closed shop rules and practices assessed for Charter purposes?

37. Under what circumstances can arbitration be used to end a strike or other form of labour conflict?

38. What is the minimum period of compulsory maternity leave?

39. In what sense is the Charter's concept of social assistance a modern one?

40. Does the Charter require a guaranteed minimum income for persons in need?

41. Does the Charter require an employment quota for disabled persons?

42. What are the Charter's provisions regarding relationship by descent?

43. What are the Charter's requirements regarding education? What about the revised Charter?

44. What are the Charter's requirements regarding foreign nationals resident in Contracting Parties (residence and work permits, etc.)?

45. Which of the rights guaranteed under the Charter extend to migrants?

46. Who is entitled to family reunion under the Charter? Under the revised Charter?

47. Under what circumstances can a foreign national be expelled from a country?

48. What restrictions on the right to strike are authorised under Article 6 para. 4?

49. Does the Charter authorise night work? For whom? Subject to what conditions? And the revised Charter?

50. What is the situation of Contracting Parties with regard to obligations they have accepted at the end of supervision cycle XIV-2?

Answers

1. Is ratification of the Charter obligatory for Council of Europe member states? Or for new member states?

Ratification of the Charter is not obligatory for either long-standing or new member states. However, such an obligation has existed since 1974 with regard to the European Convention on Human Rights (ECHR): countries must sign the ECHR on the day of their accession to the Council of Europe and ratify it one year after.

While Charter ratification is not obligatory, it is still an objective with strong political backing that has been reaffirmed on a number of occasions. For example, in May 1997, the Parliamentary Assembly launched a campaign to secure the maximum possible number of ratifications of the 1961 or the revised Charter. Still more recently, the Second Summit of Heads of State and Government, held in Strasbourg on 10 and 11 October 1997, called for the "widest possible adherence" to the Social Charter.

Applicants for Council of Europe membership must undertake to examine the Charter with a view to its ratification and, in the meantime, apply a policy consistent with its principles (opinion of the Parliamentary Assembly concerning accession applications from new states). The obligation to ratify has been accepted by a number of countries, such as Andorra and, more recently, Georgia. The latter has undertaken to ratify the Charter within three years of its accession (see Fact Sheet B – 1).

2. What are the core provisions:
   - of the Charter?
   - of the revised Charter?

a. Core provisions of the Social Charter

Seven of the articles in Part II (see Article 20.1 b), at least five of which must be accepted by Contracting Parties, form the core of the Charter:

- Article 1 (right to work),
- Article 5 (right to organise),
- Article 6 (right to bargain collectively),
- Article 12 (right to social security),
- Article 13 (right to social and medical assistance),
- Article 16 (right of the family to social, legal and economic protection),
- Article 19 (right of migrant workers and their families to protection and assistance).

b. Core provisions of the revised Social Charter

Nine of the articles in Part II (see Article A para. 1.b of Part III), at least six of which must be accepted by Contracting Parties, form the core:

– The seven articles of the Charter referred to above, plus,

– Article 7 (right of children and young persons to protection),

– Article 20 (right to equal opportunities and equal treatment in matters of employment and occupation without discrimination on the grounds of sex).

3. What is the minimum number of provisions countries are required to accept:

– **in the Charter (...Articles or ...paragraphs)?**

– **in the revised Charter (...Articles or ...paragraphs)?**

a. Social Charter:

Under Article 20 para. 1 of the Charter, countries must accept at least five of the seven core articles and at least ten articles or forty-five paragraphs of Part II.

b. Revised Social Charter:

Under Article A para. 1 of the revised Charter, countries must accept at least six of the nine core articles and at least sixteen articles or sixty-three paragraphs of Part II.

4. How many countries have accepted all the Charter's provisions? Which?

Five countries have accepted all the Charter's provisions: Belgium, France, Italy, the Netherlands and Portugal.

Spain fell into this category until 5 June 1991, when it denounced Article 8 para. 4b (prohibition of female employment in certain types of work).

So far, one country – France – has accepted all the provisions of the revised Charter.

5. How often do governments submit reports?

Under the system for submitting reports introduced in June 1997, all countries report on the same articles over the same reference period. Reports are submitted every two years on the core provisions and every four years on the others.

6. How many members does the European Committee of Social Rights have?

The European Committee of Social Rights is composed of nine members (Article 25 of the Charter and Committee of Ministers' decision in March 1994), elected by the Committee of Ministers for a six-year once renewable term.

7. What is the composition of the Governmental Committee?

The Governmental Committee comprises one representative from each of the countries that have ratified the Charter or the revised Charter.

In 1992, the Committee of Ministers decided to invite observers from central and east European member states that had signed the Charter to attend Governmental Committee meetings, in preparation for their ratification. In December 1998, the Committee of Ministers extended this invitation to all signatory states.

8. How do the social partners (employers' associations and trade unions) participate in the supervisory machinery?

Under Article 23 of the Charter, each country must send a copy of reports on accepted (Article 21) and non-accepted (Article 22) provisions to national organisations that are members of the international organisations that take part in Governmental Committee meetings. These organisations can then submit their comments on the national reports.

In addition, Article 27 of the Charter empowers the Governmental Committee to invite two international employers' and two international trade union organisations to take part in its meetings in a consultative capacity. Until now, the Union of Industrial and Employers' Confederations of Europe (UNICE), the International Organisation of Employers (IOE) and the European Trade Union Confederation (ETUC), which took over from the International Confederation of Free Trade Unions (ICFTU) and the World Confederation of Labour (WCL), have been invited to take part in Governmental Committee meetings.

9. Which supervisory machinery documents are public and when do they become so?

The following are public documents: government reports, once they have been submitted to the Council of Europe, and the conclusions of the European Committee of Social Rights, Governmental Committee reports and Committee of Ministers resolutions and recommendations, once they have been adopted.

10. What is a warning?
– who addresses it?
– in what circumstances?
– what is its legal status?

The Governmental Committee can address warnings to countries that do not comply with a Charter provision, following a negative conclusion of the European Committee of Social Rights or a repeated failure to supply information.

Fact sheet A – 8 on the Governmental Committee's working methods sets out the circumstances in which it can consider issuing a warning to a member state (see in particular section C: examination of negative conclusions):

"where there is no majority in favour of a recommendation, [the Governmental Committee] will then also take a vote on whether to address a warning to the state concerned (two-thirds majority of votes cast). If a warning follows a negative conclusion, it serves as an indication to the state that, unless it takes measures to comply with its obligations under the Charter, a recommendation will be proposed in the next part of a cycle where this provision is under examination;

in so far as the examination concerns a Contracting Party submitting its first report, the subject of the first set of conclusions of the European Committee of Social Rights, the Committee issues a warning rather than a recommendation in the case of negative conclusions. The Committee considers this approach necessary in order to give the countries concerned some time to consider and respond to the findings of the Committee of Social Rights."

Warnings have no legal status. They are more political in nature, alarm bells to warn governments that if they fail to take action a recommendation will be considered at the next supervision cycle.

11. What is a recommendation?
   - who adopts it?
   - since when?
   - what majority is required?

The Committee of Ministers is authorised to adopt recommendations.

It has had this power, one of the main developments arising from the Turin Protocol, since the twelfth supervision cycle, first part (1993), covering the reference period 1988-1989.

The Committee of Ministers' decisions are prepared by the Governmental Committee which, having regard to social policy and political considerations, selects violations of the Charter identified by the European Committee of Social Rights which should be the subject of recommendations to the governments concerned.

Two Committee of Ministers decisions have established the rules governing the adoption of Charter recommendations:
   - the first, in April 1993, restricts the right to vote when the Committee of Ministers is acting as one of the Charter's supervisory bodies to representatives of those member states that have ratified it;

– under the second, in June 1995, to be adopted a recommendation requires a two-thirds majority of deputies voting and a majority of all the Charter's Contracting Parties.

12. How many recommendations has the Committee of Ministers adopted?

To date, twenty-nine recommendations have been issued to fourteen countries. For more details, see Fact Sheet A – 10.

13. What is the Parliamentary Assembly's role in the supervisory procedure?

Under Article 28 of the Charter, the conclusions of the European Committee of Social Rights are sent to the Parliamentary Assembly for an opinion. In practice, following an exchange of letters in June 1992 between the President of the Parliamentary Assembly and the Chair of the Committee of Ministers, the Assembly withdrew from the Charter's supervisory system. It refrains from issuing opinions on the conclusions but may use them as a basis for periodical debates on social policy.

14. What forms of discrimination are prohibited by the Charter?

The Preamble to the Social Charter states that "the enjoyment of social rights should be secured without discrimination on grounds of race, colour, sex, religion, political opinion, national extraction or social origin". Any form of discrimination, whether direct or indirect (see also question 15), based on one or more of these grounds is therefore prohibited, whichever Article of the Charter is concerned. The revised Charter of 1996 extends the scope of this principle by introducing a general non-discrimination clause (Part V, Article E) which, drawing on Article 14 of the ECHR, prohibits all discrimination on grounds set out in a non-exhaustive list.

15. In what circumstances does the Charter's case law draw on the notion of indirect discrimination?

The European Committee of Social Rights considers that when a rule is applied in identical fashion to different groups of individuals – and is therefore apparently neutral – but in practice affects one group more than another, this constitutes indirect discrimination.

One example is a residence requirement for entitlement to certain rights or benefits which, although equally applicable to nationals and foreign residents, is more difficult for the latter to satisfy (see, for example, the committee's position regarding social security benefits (Article 12 para. 4), family benefits (Article 16), universal access to vocational training (Article 10) and disabled persons' access to vocational training (Article 15)).

The Committee has also ruled that certain criteria for determining wages that apply to men as well as women and therefore seem to be neutral from a sex standpoint may constitute indirect discrimination for the purposes of Article 4 para. 3 (equal pay for women and men).

16. What rights are recognised by both the Charter and the European Convention on Human Rights?

The following rights are recognised in the European Convention on Human Rights and the European Social Charter:

- prohibition of forced labour (Article 4 ECHR and Article 1 para. 2 European Social Charter);
- right to family life (Article 8 ECHR and Articles 16, 17 and 19 para. 6 Charter);
- right to organise (Article 11 ECHR and Article 5 Charter).

The two treaties also both include provisions on non-discrimination (Article 14 of the ECHR, Preamble to the Charter, Article E Part V of the revised Charter).

In addition, Articles 6 (access to the courts) and 13 (right to an effective remedy) of the ECHR include provisions which the European Committee of Social Rights has drawn on extensively when interpreting certain Charter rules (with particular regard to the right to seek a remedy in the courts, see the Committee's case law on Articles 1 para. 2 (non-discrimination in employment), 4 para. 3 (equal pay) and 13 para. 1 (right of persons in need to social and medical assistance), Article 1 of the additional Protocol (equal opportunities and treatment in employment and occupation matters) and Article 19 para. 8 (safeguards against expulsion). See also the answer to question 30.

17. What rights recognised by the United Nations Covenant on Economic, Social and Cultural Rights are not recognised by the Charter or the revised Charter?

See, for example:

- Article 11 para. 2 of the Covenant (right to freedom from hunger), which sets out in detail the measures the Contracting Parties are required to take to safeguard this right (sub-paras a and b), whereas this right does not exist as such in the Charter. However, the latter does include key provisions concerned with combating poverty: Article 13 (right to social and medical assistance) requires Contracting Parties to take all possible steps to abolish or reduce need. This Article is supplemented by Article 30 of the revised Charter (right to protection against poverty and social exclusion), under which the parties undertake "to take measures within the framework of an overall and co-ordinated approach to promote the effective access of persons who live or risk living in a situation of social exclusion or poverty, as well as their families".

- Article 15 (participation in cultural life and the diffusion of science and culture).
- Article 1 (right of self-determination).
- Article 5 (prohibition of abuse of law) and Article 10 (freely consented marriage).

18. What are the cultural rights recognised by the Charter?

The Social Charter only covers this type of right in a limited and, sometimes, indirect fashion. For example, Article 10 covers the right to vocational training, which implies a right to initial training and thus to education.

Moreover, a certain number of Charter rights are concerned with full participation in social – and thus cultural – life, for example, Article 4 of Protocol No. 1, which calls for appropriate measures "to enable elderly persons to remain full members of society for as long as possible", such as granting them adequate resources to enable them to play an active part in public, social and cultural life, or Article 15 para. 3 of the revised Charter, which is concerned with the full social integration and participation of disabled persons in the life of the community by giving them access to cultural activities and leisure.

Article 17 of the revised Charter makes it obligatory to provide free primary and secondary education.

Article 19 paras. 11 and 12 of the revised Charter contain provisions on language teaching for migrants and their families (language of the host country and their mother tongue).

Finally, Article 30 of the revised Charter refers to culture in the context of protection against poverty and social exclusion.

19. What rights are included in the Additional Protocol of 1988?

The Additional Protocol adds a series of rights in four articles:
- Article 1: right to equal opportunities and equal treatment in matters of employment and occupation without discrimination on the grounds of sex;
- Article 2: employees' right to information and consultation;
- Article 3: employees' right to take part in the determination and improvement of their working conditions and working environment;
- Article 4: elderly persons' right to social protection.

20. What are the amended provisions in the revised Charter?

The amendments in the revised Social Charter concern the following articles:
- Article 2 (right to just conditions of work);

- Article 3 (right to safe and healthy working conditions);
- Article 7 (right of children and young persons to protection);
- Article 8 (right of employed women to protection of maternity);
- Article 10 (right to vocational training);
- Article 12 (right to social security);
- Article 15 (right of persons with disabilities to independence, social integration and participation in the life of the community);
- Article 17 (right of children and young persons to social, legal and economic protection);
- Article 19 (right of migrant workers and their families to protection and assistance).

For more details see Fact Sheet A – 4.

21. What are the new rights in the revised Charter?

The following new rights are included in the revised Charter:
- right to protection in cases of termination of employment (Article 24);
- right of workers to the protection of their claims in the event of the insolvency of their employer (Article 25);
- right to dignity at work (Article 26);
- right of workers with family responsibilities to equal opportunities and equal treatment (Article 27);
- right of workers' representatives to protection in the undertaking and facilities to be accorded to them (Article 28);
- right to information and consultation in collective redundancy procedures (Article 29);
- right to protection against poverty and social exclusion (Article 30);
- right to housing (Article 31).

For more details see Fact Sheet A – 4.

22. Who can lodge collective complaints?

Collective complaints may be lodged by:
- international employers' associations and trade unions taking part in the Governmental Committee's activities in accordance with Article 27 para. 2 of the Charter, that is UNICE, IOE and ETUC;
- other international non-governmental organisations with Council of Europe consultative status and registered on a special list drawn up for that purpose by the Governmental Committee;

(for more details see Fact Sheet A – 13).
- the national employers' organisations and trade unions of the country concerned;

– In addition, any country can make a written declaration to the Council of Europe's Secretary General authorising national non-governmental organisations with competence in this field to lodge complaints against it.

23. What is the Governmental Committee's role in the collective complaints procedure?

The Governmental Committee is consulted when the following conditions are met (Article 9 para. 2 of Protocol No. 3):

– when the Contracting Party concerned so requests;

– when the report of the European Committee of Social Rights raises new issues;

– when the Committee of Ministers so decides by a two-thirds majority of the Charter's Contracting Parties.

24. What is the Committee of Ministers' role in the collective complaints procedure?

The Committee of Ministers becomes involved at the end of the collective complaints procedure by adopting either a recommendation or a resolution:

if the European Committee of Social Rights concludes that there has been a Charter violation, the Committee of Ministers adopts a recommendation. This decision is taken by a two-thirds majority of those voting, with only Contracting Parties to the Charter taking part in the vote;

– if the European Committee of Social Rights concludes that there has not been a Charter violation, the Committee of Ministers adopts a resolution by a majority of those voting. Such a resolution ends the procedure.

25. What are the admissibility conditions for collective complaints?

Article 4 of Protocol No. 3 lays down three main admissibility conditions:

– the complaint must be lodged in writing;

– it must relate to a provision of the Charter accepted by the Contracting Party concerned;

– it must indicate in what respect the provision has not been satisfactorily applied.

In addition, para. 31 of the explanatory report states that the European Committee of Social Rights should take account of the following factors:

– a complaint may be declared admissible even if a similar case has been submitted to another national or international body;

- the fact that the substance of a complaint has been examined as part of the "normal" government reports procedure does not in itself constitute a barrier to the complaint's admissibility;
- complaints may not relate to individual situations.

The European Committee's Rules of Procedure also contain relevant provisions (see articles 19 to 21):

- complaints must be signed by a person competent to represent the claimant organisation;
- complaints made by European trade unions, employers' organisations or NGOs must be submitted in one of the Council of Europe's official languages (English or French); complaints made by national organisations may be submitted in non-official languages (see also the first admissibility decision: Complaint No. 1/1998, decision of 10 March 1999, and the first inadmissibility decision: Complaint No. 3/1999, decision of 3 October 1999.

26. According to the European Committee of Social Rights, what rights have to be enshrined in law to be effective?

The Committee requires statutory enforcement of the following rights:

- Article 1 para. 2: countries must enact legislation prohibiting discrimination between women and men in employment;
- Article 3: governments must introduce health and safety regulations and measures to monitor their application;
- Article 4 para. 3: countries must make it a statutory obligation for women and men to receive the same pay not only for the same work but also for work of equal value;
- Article 7 para. 1: states must adopt legislation to prohibit the employment of children under fifteen years of age, except in certain tasks classified as "light work";
- Article 8 para. 1: female employees must have a statutory right to paid maternity leave. Moreover, under Article 8 para. 4, there must be legislation prohibiting the employment of women workers in underground mining and on other work deemed to be dangerous, unhealthy or arduous;
- Article 13: anyone in need must have guaranteed entitlement to public assistance, with a right of appeal to an independent body;
- Article 19 para. 8: national legislation must provide for a certain number of safeguards against expulsion, particularly an effective right of appeal to the courts or another independent body;
- Article 1 of Protocol No. 1: to ensure equal opportunities and equal treatment in matters of employment and occupation without discrimination on the grounds of sex, countries must provide for a whole series of statutory rights: the right of employees of both sexes to institute proceedings in the courts or with any other com-

petent body; the right to have conditions incompatible with the non-discrimination principle declared null and void; appropriate safeguards against discriminatory or retaliatory measures; and the right to have discriminatory situations put right or, in the case of dismissal, re-employment and compensation for any financial loss in the intervening period, with a reduction in the burden of proof.

27. What provisions of the Charter deemed to be respected if the rules that implement them apply to at least 80% of the population concerned?

Under Article 33 of the Charter, paras. 1 to 5 of Article 2 (right to just conditions of work), paras. 4, 6 and 7 of Article 7 (right of children and young persons to protection) and paras. 1 to 4 of Article 10 (right to vocational training) are considered to be effective when they are applied to the "great majority" of the employees concerned (set at 80%).

28. What persons are protected by the Charter (its scope *ratione personae*)?

Countries must apply the Charter to their nationals and to the nationals of other Contracting Parties lawfully resident or working regularly within their territory.

Moreover, Contracting Parties are required to grant to refugees, as defined in the Geneva Convention of 28th July 1951 relating to the Status of Refugees and lawfully staying in their territory, as favourable treatment as possible (Appendix to the Charter: scope of the Social Charter in terms of persons protected, paras. 1 and 2).

Protocol No. 1 and the revised Charter have extended this treatment to stateless persons as defined in the New York Convention of 28 September 1954.

Certain provisions go beyond these restrictive conditions governing the Charter's application to foreigners. These provisions apply to foreigners who, while they must be nationals of one of the Charter's Contracting Parties, are not resident in the territory of the country concerned. The relevant provisions are:

– Article 12 para. 4, which provides for equal treatment in respect of social security not only for residents but also for those who have resided in the territory of a Contracting Party and have thereby acquired rights (for example, entitlement to an old age pension), as well as those who have resided in the territory of several Contracting Parties;

– Article 13 para. 4, which provides for equal treatment for residents in respect of social assistance but also for a certain form of social assistance for those lawfully in the territory of a Contracting Party without residing there;

– Article 18, which provides for the simplification of formalities regarding work or residence permits for foreign nationals, which applies before they enter the country (at least in the case of the first permits issued to them);

– Article 19, which requires co-operation between social services when persons leave their country and during their journey; clearly, these provisions apply to migrants who are not – yet – resident in the country concerned.

29. To what extent are foreigners eligible for social assistance?

Foreigners have the same entitlement to social and medical assistance as a country's nationals if they are nationals of a Charter Contracting Party and lawfully resident or working regularly in the country where they apply for assistance.

This right is provided for in Article 13 paras. 1 and 4. In the case of countries that have accepted the two provisions, the European Committee of Social Rights examines respect for this right from the standpoint of Article 13 para. 1.

Article 13 para. 4 goes further in that it concerns any national of a Contracting Party to the Charter "lawfully within" the territory of another Contracting Party. This category extends beyond persons residing or working to others, such as students or tourists, who are lawfully in a country without residing there.

Under Article 13 para. 4, the last named group are also eligible for social assistance. By definition, this assistance is limited according to their situation, but must cover urgent needs. Moreover, assistance for persons temporarily in a country is limited in time and there is the possibility of repatriating the individuals concerned to their country of origin, subject to the conditions and constraints provided for in the 1953 Convention.

30. What provisions of the Charter entail a right of appeal to the domestic courts?

Articles 1 para. 2 (non-discrimination in employment), 4 para. 3 (equal pay) and 13 para. 1 (right of persons in need to social and medical assistance), Article 1 of the additional protocol (equal opportunities and equal treatment in matters of employment and occupation) and Article 18 para. 8 (safeguards against expulsion) have been interpreted by the European Committee of Social Rights as entailing a right of appeal to the domestic courts.

31. How does the European Committee of Social Rights monitor Article 1 para. 1 of the Charter: "right to work – full employment"?

The Committee has interpreted this provision as an obligation of means rather than results. Its purpose is not to secure countries' recognition of an individual right to work but the adoption of economic policies aimed at improving the employment situation, coupled with the necessary measures to achieve this. The Committee has not adopted conclusions on this paragraph since the 8th supervision cycle but examines and comments on the changes that have occurred and the progress achieved.

32. How many public holidays does the Charter require?

Article 2 para. 2 of the Charter stipulates that there should be public holidays but does not say how many days should be granted. The European Committee of Social Rights has never specified a minimum number. Nevertheless, having regard to the circumstances of the countries that have ratified the Charter it has concluded that between 6 and 17 days are appropriate to meet the requirements of this provision.

33. What are the conditions for a country to be in compliance with Article 4 para. 3, which requires equal pay for women and men for work of equal value?

To ensure that this right is effectively exercised, Contracting Parties are required to make provision for it in their legislation. They must establish objective criteria for assessing the work concerned based on comparisons from outside the enterprise and encourage higher wages in sectors with a high percentage of female employees, which are generally less well paid. Finally, they must guarantee effective protection in the form of adequate remedies to secure the removal of any clauses in collective agreements or individual contracts that are incompatible with the equal pay principle.

34. What is meant by work of equal value, as provided for in Article 4 para. 3 of the Charter?

Under Article 4 para. 3, countries are required to recognise the right of male and female employees to equal pay for work of equal value. In other words, equal pay must apply not only to the same work but also to work of equal value, which necessitates the establishment of objective criteria for assessing jobs and comparing their respective values.

35. What, according to the Charter, is the "decency threshold" for remuneration?

Under Article 4 para. 1, Contracting Parties are required "to recognise the right of workers to a remuneration such as will give them and their families a decent standard of living". A decent standard of living is taken to mean that workers and their families must be able to satisfy their basic needs, such as food and accommodation, and benefit from improvements to their living conditions so that they can satisfy their cultural and social needs and the requirement of access to education.

The Committee has established a "decency threshold" of 60% of the average annual net wage, below which wages cannot be deemed to be compatible with the Charter.

36. How are closed shop rules and practices assessed for Charter purposes?

Legislation authorising closed shop rules or practices is considered to be in breach of Article 5 of the Charter. This provision is deemed to cover negative as well as positive aspects of the right to organise. The freedom to join a trade union must be guaranteed, but this also implies that there can be no obligation in practice to become or remain a trade union member.

37. Under what circumstances can arbitration be used to end a strike or other form of labour conflict?

Arbitration can normally only be used for these purposes with the agreement of both parties to the conflict. However, it may be imposed against one of the parties' will in specific cases provided for in Article 31 of the Charter, that is when it is necessary in a democratic society for the protection of the rights and freedoms of others or for the protection of public interest, national security, public health, or morals.

38. What is the minimum period of compulsory maternity leave?

Under Article 8 para. 1, maternity leave must be for a minimum of twelve weeks, to be taken before and after childbirth. The European Committee of Social Rights has ruled that this Charter provision authorises those concerned to waive entitlement to part of this leave, other than a minimum of six weeks' cessation of work following the birth.

39. In what sense is the Charter's concept of social assistance a modern one?

Article 13 of the Charter makes social assistance an individual right for everyone in need. As such, it differs from the traditional view of assistance as a moral duty based on charity.

40. Does the Charter require a guaranteed minimum income for persons in need?

Article 13 does not give any indication of the form that social assistance should take. However, according to the European Committee of Social Rights, the entire population should potentially benefit from social assistance, a requirement that is satisfied by the introduction of a general guaranteed minimum income. Such systems now exist in the majority of countries that have ratified the Charter. In others however there is no flat-rate payment or single allowance, the level of assistance being determined according to everyone's specific needs.

41. Does the Charter require an employment quota for disabled persons?

Under Article 15 para. 2 of the Charter, Contracting Parties undertake to institute placement and other employment measures for disabled persons. The Charter does not require an employment quota for disabled persons but leaves it to individual countries to decide what methods to use to find work for disabled persons. The European Committee of Social Rights then considers the adequacy and appropriateness of the measures adopted when deciding whether or not the situation is in compliance with Article 15.

42. What are the Charter's provisions regarding relationship by descent?

The European Committee of Social Rights is concerned with the establishment of relationship by descent in the context of establishing natural paternity or maternity, legitimation and adoption. In all these areas, the Charter stipulates that children born within and outside of marriage should have equal access to the relevant procedures. More specifically, in the area of adoption the European Committee has interpreted the Charter as requiring the maintenance of the links between children, their families of origin and their adoptive families. More recently, the Committee has examined adoption procedures from the standpoint of the parents' involvement on an equal footing.

43. What are the Charter's requirements regarding education? What about the revised Charter?

The Social Charter does not include any explicit right to education or instruction. However, it does contain a series of provisions concerned with such a right. In particular, prohibiting children under fifteen from working, other than light work that does not interfere with their studies, is a fundamental element of a right to education. In addition, Article 9 of the Charter provides for a right to vocational guidance, which particularly concerns school age children.

Article 10 para. 1 of the Charter provides for rights both to technical and vocational training and to access to higher technical and university education, based solely on individual aptitude.

Article 17 of the revised Charter provides explicitly for free primary and secondary education as well as state encouragement for regular attendance at schools.

44. What are the Charter's requirements regarding foreign nationals resident in Contracting Parties (residence and work permits, etc.)?

The Social Charter does not provide for freedom of establishment. Countries are still free to determine their own immigration policies. However, they have to liberalise and simplify the procedures governing the admission of foreigners into their territory.

45. Which of the rights guaranteed under the Charter extend to migrants?

All the rights enshrined in the Charter apply to migrant workers and their families if they are nationals of Contracting Parties and are legally resident or working regularly in the territory of the Contracting Party concerned. The Charter also offers migrant workers special protection: Article 18 gives migrant workers and their families the right to engage in a gainful occupation in the territory of other Contracting Parties while Article 19 gives them the right to protection and assistance.

46. Who is entitled to family reunion under the Charter? Under the revised Charter?

Under Article 19 para. 6 of the Charter, Contracting Parties undertake to facilitate the family reunion of foreign workers permitted to establish themselves in their territory. The appendix to the Charter defines such families as including at least the wife and dependent children under the age of twenty-one years.

The European Committee of Social Rights has specified that the term "worker" extends to women as well as men and that as a result the definition of the family of a foreign worker in the Appendix to the Charter includes the dependent children (but not the husband) of a female worker.

The definition of the family of a migrant worker has been modified in the revised Charter. According to the appendix to Article 19 para. 6, the family of a foreign worker no longer only extends to the worker's wife but now includes a male or female worker's spouse. Moreover, the children admitted for family reunion purposes are the dependent unmarried children, as long as the latter are considered to be minors by the receiving state.

47. Under what circumstances can a foreign national be expelled from a country?

According to Article 19 para. 8, workers legally resident in a Contracting Party can only be expelled if they endanger national security or offend against public interest or morality.

These grounds must be strictly interpreted: in particular, a threat to "public health" would only justify an expulsion on grounds of danger to the public interest if the individual concerned refused to undergo appropriate treatment.

Where an expulsion order is made, there must be a right of appeal to a court or other independent body.

48. What restrictions on the right to strike are authorised under Article 6 para. 4?

It is not contrary to the provisions of Article 6 para. 4 to prohibit strikes for certain categories of civil servant, including members of the police and armed forces, judges and senior officials, so long as this does not amount to a total abolition of the right to strike for all categories of civil servants, and persons providing essential public services, provided the restrictions are compatible with Article 31 of the Charter.

49. Does the Charter authorise night work? For whom? Subject to what conditions? And the revised Charter?

The Social Charter does not prohibit night work but does require Contracting Parties to regulate the employment of women workers on night work in industrial employment (Article 8 para. 4 a).

The revised Charter reduces the personal scope of this obligation since according to Article 8 para. 4, parties are only required to regulate the employment in night work of pregnant women, women who have recently given birth and women nursing their infants. However, under Article 2 para. 7 men and women performing night work should benefit from measures which take account of the special nature of the work.

50. What is the situation of Contracting Parties with regard to obligations they have accepted at the end of supervision cycle XIV-2?

See Fact Sheet A – 12.

Appendices

Appendix 1
Situation of signatures and ratifications of the Charter, its Protocols and the revised Charter

Situation at 1 July 2000

Member states	1961 European Social Charter		1988 Additional Protocol		1991 Amending Protocol		1995 Collective Complaints Protocol		1996 Revised European Social Charter	
	Signature	Ratification	Signature	Ratification	Signature	Ratification	Signature	Ratification	Signature	Ratification
Albania	–								21/09/98	
Andorra	–	–	–	–	–	–	–	–	–	–
Austria	22/07/63	29/10/69	04/12/90	–	07/05/92	13/07/95	07/05/99	–	07/05/99	–
Belgium	18/10/61	16/10/90	20/05/92	–	22/10/91	**	14/05/96	–	03/05/96	–
Bulgaria	–	–	–	–	–	–	–	–	21/09/98	07/06/00
Croatia	08/03/99	–	08/03/99	–	08/03/99	–	08/03/99	–	–	–
Cyprus	22/05/67	07/03/68	05/05/88	–	21/10/91	01/06/93	09/11/95	06/08/96	03/05/96	–
Czech Republic	27/05/92*	3/11/99	27/05/92*	17/11/99	27/05/92*	17/11/99	–	–	–	–
Denmark	18/10/61	03/03/65	27/08/96	27/08/96	–	**	09/11/95	–	03/05/96	–
Estonia	–	–	–	–	–	–	–	–	04/05/98	–
Finland	09/02/90	29/04/91	09/02/90	29/04/91	16/03/92	18/08/94	09/11/95	17/07/98	03/05/96	–
France	18/10/61	09/03/73	22/06/89	(2)	21/10/91	24/05/95	09/11/95	07/05/99	03/05/96	07/05/99
Georgia	–	–	–	–	–	–	–	–	–	–
Germany	18/10/61	27/01/65	05/05/88	–	–	**	–	–	–	–
Greece	18/10/61	06/06/84	05/05/88	18/06/98	29/11/91	12/09/96	18/06/98	18/06/98	03/05/96	–

Member states	1961 European Social Charter		1988 Additional Protocol		1991 Amending Protocol		1995 Collective Complaints Protocol		1996 Revised European Social Charter	
	Signature	Ratification	Signature	Ratification	Signature	Ratification	Signature	Ratification	Signature	Ratification
Hungary	13/12/91	08/07/99	-	-	13/12/91	**	-	-	-	-
Iceland	15/01/76	15/01/76	05/05/88	-	-	**	-	-	04/11/98	-
Ireland	18/10/61	07/10/64	-	-	14/05/97	14/05/97	-	-	-	-
Italy	18/10/61	22/10/65	05/05/88	26/05/94	21/10/91	27/01/95	09/11/95	03/11/97	03/05/96	05/07/99
Latvia	29/05/97	-	29/05/97	-	29/05/97	-	-	-	-	-
Liechtenstein	09/10/91	-	-	-	-	-	-	-	-	-
Lithuania	-	-	-	-	-	-	-	-	08/09/97	-
Luxembourg	18/10/61	10/10/91	05/05/88	-	21/10/91	**	-	-	11/02/98	-
Malta	26/05/88	04/10/88	-	-	21/10/91	16/02/94	-	-	-	-
Moldova	-	-	-	-	-	-	-	-	03/11/98	-
Netherlands	18/10/61	22/04/80	14/06/90	05/08/92	21/10/91	01/06/93	-	-	-	-
Norway	18/10/61	26/10/62	10/12/93	10/12/93	21/10/91	21/10/91	20/03/97	20/03/97	-	-
Poland	26/11/91	25/06/97	-	-	18/04/97	25/06/97	-	-	-	-
Portugal	01/06/82	30/09/91	-	-	24/02/92	08/03/93	09/11/95	20/03/98	03/05/96	-
Romania	04/10/94	(1)	-	(2)	-	-	-	-	14/05/97	07/05/99
Russia	-	-	-	-	-	-	-	-	-	-

Member states	1961 European Social Charter		1988 Additional Protocol		1991 Amending Protocol		1995 Collective Complaints Protocol		1996 Revised European Social Charter	
	Signature	Ratification	Signature	Ratification	Signature	Ratification	Signature	Ratification	Signature	Ratification
San Marino	-	-	-	-	-	-	-	-	-	-
Slovakia	27/05/92*	22/06/98	27/05/92*	22/06/98	27/05/92*	22/06/98	18/11/99	-	18/11/99	-
Slovenia	11/10/97	(1)	11/10/97	(2)	11/10/97	-	11/10/97	(3)	11/10/97	07/05/99
Spain	27/04/78	06/05/80	05/05/88	24/01/00	21/10/91	27/01/00	-	-	-	-
Sweden	18/10/61	17/12/62	05/05/88	05/05/89	21/10/91	18/03/92	09/11/95	29/05/98	03/05/96	29/05/98
Switzerland	06/05/76	-	-	-	-	-	-	-	-	-
"Former Yug. Rep. of Macedonia"	05/05/98	-	05/05/98	-	05/05/98	-	-	-	-	-
Turkey	18/10/61	24/11/89	05/05/98	-	-	**	-	-	-	-
Ukraine	02/05/96	-	-	-	-	-	-	-	07/05/99	-
United Kingdom	18/10/61	11/07/62	-	-	21/10/91	**	-	-	07/11/97	-

*   Date of signature by the Czech and Slovak Federal Republic.
**   State whose acceptance is necessary for the entry into force of the Protocol.
(1) State having ratified the revised Social Charter.
(2) State having accepted the rights (or certain rights) guaranteed by the Protocol in the framework of the revised Social Charter.
(3) State having accepted the collective complaints procedure by a declaration made in application of Article D para. 2 of Part IV of the revised Social Charter.

239

Appendix 2
Acceptance of the provisions of the Charter and the revised Chart

Table showing details of the accepted provisions of the European Social Charter

Provision of the Charter	Austria	Belgium	Cyprus	Czech Republic	Denmark	Finland	Germany	Greece
Article 1 (1)	■	■	■	■	■	■	■	■
Article 1 (2)	■	■	■	■	■	■	■	■
Article 1 (3)	■	■	■	■	■	■	■	■
Article 1 (4)	■	■	■		■	■	■	■
Article 2 (1)		■	■	■		■	■	■
Article 2 (2)	■	■		■	■	■	■	■
Article 2 (3)	■	■		■	■	■	■	■
Article 2 (4)	■	■		■		■	■	■
Article 2 (5)	■	■	■	■	■	■	■	■
Article 3 (1)	■	■	■	■	■		■	■
Article 3 (2)	■	■	■	■	■		■	■
Article 3 (3)	■	■	■	■	■	■	■	■
Article 4 (1)	■	■	■		■		■	■
Article 4 (2)	■	■		■	■	■	■	■
Article 4 (3)	■	■	■	■	■	■	■	■
Article 4 (4)		■		■				■
Article 4 (5)	■			■	■		■	■
Article 5	■	■	■	■	■	■	■	
Article 6 (1)	■	■	■	■	■	■	■	
Article 6 (2)	■	■	■	■	■	■	■	

accepted ■ not accepted □

Hungary	Iceland	Ireland	Luxembourg	Malta	Netherlands*	Norway	Poland	Portugal	Slovakia	Spain	Turkey	United Kingdom
■	■	■	■	■	■	■	■	■	■	■	■	■
■	■	■	■	■	■	■	■	■	■	■	■	■
■	■	■	■	■	■	■	■	■	■	■	■	■
■	■	■	■	■	■	■	■	■	■	■	■	■
■	■	■	■	■	■	■	■	■	■	■	□	□
■	□	■	■	■	■	■	□	■	■	■	□	■
■	■	■	■	■	■	■	■	■	■	■	□	■
■	□	■	■	□	■	■	■	■	■	■	□	■
■	■	■	■	■	■	■	■	■	■	■	□	■
■	■	■	■	■	■	■	■	■	■	■	□	■
■	■	■	■	■	■	■	■	■	■	■	□	■
■	■	■	■	■	■	■	■	■	■	■	□	■
□	■	■	■	■	■	■	□	■	■	■	■	■
□	■	■	■	■	■	■	■	■	■	■	■	■
□	■	□	■	■	■	■	■	■	■	■	■	□
□	■	■	□	■	■	■	■	■	■	■	■	■
□	■	■	■	■	■	■	■	■	■	■	■	■
■	■	■	■	■	■	■	■	■	■	■	□	■
■	■	■	■	■	■	■	■	■	■	■	□	■
■	■	■	■	■	■	■	■	■	■	■	□	■

Provision of the Charter	Austria	Belgium	Cyprus	Czech Republic	Denmark	Finland	Germany	Greece
Article 6 (3)	■	■	■	■	■	■	■	
Article 6 (4)		■	■	■	■	■	■	
Article 7 (1)		■	■	■		■	■	■
Article 7 (2)	■	■		■	■	■	■	■
Article 7 (3)	■	■	■	■		■	■	■
Article 7 (4)	■	■		■		■	■	■
Article 7 (5)	■	■		■		■	■	■
Article 7 (6)	■	■	■	■		■	■	■
Article 7 (7)	■	■	■	■		■	■	■
Article 7 (8)	■	■	■	■		■	■	■
Article 7 (9)	■	■		■			■	■
Article 7 (10)	■	■	■	■	■		■	■
Article 8 (1)	■	■	■	■	■		■	■
Article 8 (2)	■	■	■	■		■		■
Article 8 (3)	■	■		■	■	■		■
Article 8 (4)		■	■	■	■	■		■
Article 9	■	■	■		■	■	■	■
Article 10 (1)	■	■			■	■	■	■
Article 10 (2)	■	■			■	■	■	■
Article 10 (3)	■	■			■	■	■	■
Article 10 (4)	■	■			■	■		■

Hungary	Iceland	Ireland	Luxembourg	Malta	Netherlands*	Norway	Poland	Portugal	Slovakia	Spain	Turkey	United Kingdom

1. Spain has not been bound by sub-paragraph *b* of this provision since 5 June 1991.
2. Only the provisions of paragraph 4, sub-paragraphs *a* and *d* have been accepted.

Provision of the Charter	Austria	Belgium	Cyprus	Czech Republic	Denmark	Finland	Germany	Greece
Article 11 (1)	■	■	■	■	■	■	■	■
Article 11 (2)	■	■	■	■	■	■	■	■
Article 11 (3)	■	■	■	■	■	■	■	■
Article 12 (1)	■	■	■	■	■	■	■	■
Article 12 (2)	■	■	■	■	■	■	■	■
Article 12 (3)	■	■	■	■	■	■	■	■
Article 12 (4)	■	■	■	■	■	■	■	■
Article 13 (1)	■	■		■	■	■	■	■
Article 13 (2)	■	■		■	■	■	■	■
Article 13 (3)	■	■		■	■	■	■	■
Article 13 (4)	■	■		■	■	■	■	■
Article 14 (1)	■	■	■	■	■	■	■	■
Article 14 (2)	■	■	■	■	■	■	■	■
Article 15 (1)	■	■	■		■	■	■	■
Article 15 (2)	■	■	■	■	■	■	■	■
Article 16	■	■	■	■	■	■	■	■
Article 17	■	■	■	■	■	■	■	■
Article 18 (1)	■	■		■	■	■	■	■
Article 18 (2)	■	■			■	■	■	■
Article 18 (3)		■			■	■	■	■
Article 18 (4)	■	■		■	■	■	■	■
Article 19 (1)	■	■	■	■		■	■	■
Article 19 (2)	■	■	■	■		■	■	■

Hungary	Iceland	Ireland	Luxembourg	Malta	Netherlands*	Norway	Poland	Portugal	Slovakia	Spain	Turkey	United Kingdom

Provision of the Charter	Austria	Belgium	Cyprus	Czech Republic	Denmark	Finland	Germany	Greece
Article 19 (3)	■	■				■	■	■
Article 19 (4)		■	■			■	■	■
Article 19 (5)	■	■	■			■	■	■
Article 19 (6)	■	■	■			■	■	■
Article 19 (7)	■	■	■			■	■	■
Article 19 (8)	■	■	■			■	■	■
Article 19 (9)	■	■	■	■			■	■
Article 19 (10)		■	■			■		■

* With respect to the Netherlands Antilles and Aruba, the Kingdom of the Netherlands has accepted

Table showing details of the accepted provisions of the 1988 Additional Protocol[1]

Provision of the Protocol	Czech Republic	Denmark	Finland	Greece	Netherlands	Norway	Slovakia	Spain
Article 1	■	■	■	■	■	■	■	■
Article 2	■	■	■	■	■	■	■	■
Article 3	■	■	■	■	■	■	■	■
Article 4	■	■	■	■		■	■	■

1. The provisions of the 1988 Additional Protocol are included in the revised European Social Charter: Articles 1 to 4 of the Protocol correspond to Articles 20 to 23 of the revised Charter.

Hungary	Iceland	Ireland	Luxembourg	Malta	Netherlands*	Norway	Poland	Portugal	Slovakia	Spain	Turkey	United Kingdom
		■	■		■	■	■	■		■	■	■
		■	■		■	■	■	■		■	■	■
		■	■		■	■	■	■		■	■	■
		■	■		■	■	■	■		■	■	■
		■	■		■	■	■	■		■	■	■
		■	■		■		■	■		■	■	■
		■	■		■	■	■	■		■	■	■
		■	■		■	■	■	■		■	■	■

Articles 1, 5, 6, and 16 and Article 1 of the Additional Protocol.

Table showing details of the accepted provisions of the revised European Social Charter

■ accepted   □ not accepted

Provision of the revised Charter	Bulgaria	France	Italy	Romania	Slovenia	Sweden
Article 1 (1)	■	■	■	■	■	■
Article 1 (2)	■	■	■	■	■	■
Article 1 (3)	■	■	■	■	■	■
Article 1 (4)	■	■	■	■	■	■
Article 2 (1)	□	■	■	■	■	□
Article 2 (2)	■	■	■	■	■	□
Article 2 (3)	□	■	■	□	■	■
Article 2 (4)	■	■	■	■	■	□
Article 2 (5)	■	■	■	■	■	■
Article 2 (6)	■	■	■	■	■	■
Article 2 (7)	■	■	■	■	■	□
Article 3 (1)	■	■	■	■	■	■
Article 3 (2)	■	■	■	■	■	■
Article 3 (3)	■	■	■	■	■	■
Article 3 (4)	■	■	■	□	■	□
Article 4 (1)	□	■	■	■	■	■
Article 4 (2)	■	■	■	■	■	□
Article 4 (3)	■	■	■	■	■	■
Article 4 (4)	■	■	■	■	■	■
Article 4 (5)	■	■	■	■	■	□
Article 5	■	■	■	■	■	■

Provision of the revised Charter	Bulgaria	France	Italy	Romania	Slovenia	Sweden
Article 6 (1)	■	■	■	■	■	■
Article 6 (2)	■	■	■	■	■	■
Article 6 (3)	■	■	■	■	■	■
Article 6 (4)	■	■	■	■	■	■
Article 7 (1)	■	■	■	■	■	■
Article 7 (2)	■	■	■	■	■	■
Article 7 (3)	■	■	■	■	■	■
Article 7 (4)	■	■	■	■	■	■
Article 7 (5)	■	■	■	■	■	
Article 7 (6)	■	■	■	■	■	
Article 7 (7)	■	■	■	■	■	■
Article 7 (8)	■	■	■	■	■	■
Article 7 (9)	■	■	■	■	■	■
Article 7 (10)	■	■	■	■	■	■
Article 8 (1)	■	■	■	■	■	■
Article 8 (2)	■	■	■	■	■	
Article 8 (3)	■	■	■	■	■	■
Article 8 (4)	■	■	■	■	■	
Article 8 (5)	■	■	■	■	■	
Article 9		■	■	■	■	■
Article 10 (1)		■	■		■	■
Article 10 (2)		■	■		■	■
Article 10 (3)		■	■		■	■
Article 10 (4)		■	■		■	■

Provision of the revised Charter	Bulgaria	France	Italy	Romania	Slovenia	Sweden
Article 10 (5)		■	■		■	■
Article 11 (1)	■	■	■	■	■	■
Article 11 (2)	■	■	■	■	■	■
Article 11 (3)	■	■	■	■	■	■
Article 12 (1)	■	■	■	■	■	■
Article 12 (2)		■	■	■	■	■
Article 12 (3)	■	■	■	■	■	■
Article 12 (4)		■	■	■	■	
Article 13 (1)	■	■	■	■		■
Article 13 (2)	■	■	■	■	■	■
Article 13 (3)	■	■	■	■	■	■
Article 13 (4)		■	■			■
Article 14 (1)	■	■	■		■	■
Article 14 (2)	■	■	■		■	■
Article 15 (1)		■	■	■	■	■
Article 15 (2)		■	■	■	■	■
Article 15 (3)		■	■		■	■
Article 16	■	■	■	■	■	■
Article 17 (1)		■	■	■	■	■
Article 17 (2)	■	■	■	■	■	■
Article 18 (1)		■	■		■	■
Article 18 (2)		■	■			■
Article 18 (3)		■	■	■	■	■
Article 18 (4)	■	■	■	■	■	■

Provision of the revised Charter	Bulgaria	France	Italy	Romania	Slovenia	Sweden
Article 19 (1)		■	■		■	■
Article 19 (2)		■	■		■	■
Article 19 (3)		■	■		■	■
Article 19 (4)		■	■		■	■
Article 19 (5)		■	■		■	■
Article 19 (6)		■	■		■	■
Article 19 (7)		■	■	■	■	■
Article 19 (8)		■	■		■	■
Article 19 (9)		■	■		■	■
Article 19 (10)		■	■		■	■
Article 19 (11)		■	■		■	■
Article 19 (12)		■	■		■	■
Article 20	■	■	■	■	■	■
Article 21	■	■	■	■	■	■
Article 22	■	■	■		■	■
Article 23		■	■	■	■	■
Article 24	■	■	■	■	■	
Article 25	■	■			■	■
Article 26 (1)	■	■	■	■	■	■
Article 26 (2)	■	■	■	■	■	■
Article 27 (1)		■	■		■	■
Article 27 (2)	■	■	■	■	■	■
Article 27 (3)	■	■	■		■	■
Article 28	■	■	■	■	■	

Provision of the revised Charter	Bulgaria	France	Italy	Romania	Slovenia	Sweden
Article 29	■	■	■	■	■	■
Article 30		■	■		■	■
Article 31 (1)		■	■		■	■
Article 31 (2)		■	■		■	■
Article 31 (3)		■	■		■	■

Sales agents for publications of the Council of Europe
Agents de vente des publications du Conseil de l'Europe

AUSTRALIA/AUSTRALIE
Hunter Publications, 58A, Gipps Street
AUS-3066 COLLINGWOOD, Victoria
Tel.: (61) 3 9417 5361
Fax: (61) 3 9419 7154
E-mail: Sales@hunter-pubs.com.au
http://www.hunter-pubs.com.au

AUSTRIA/AUTRICHE
Gerold und Co., Graben 31
A-1011 WIEN 1
Tel.: (43) 1 533 5014
Fax: (43) 1 533 5014 18
E-mail: buch@gerold.telecom.at
http://www.gerold.at

BELGIUM/BELGIQUE
La Librairie européenne SA
50, avenue A. Jonnart
B-1200 BRUXELLES 20
Tel.: (32) 2 734 0281
Fax: (32) 2 735 0860
E-mail: info@libeurop.be
http://www.libeurop.be

Jean de Lannoy
202, avenue du Roi
B-1190 BRUXELLES
Tel.: (32) 2 538 4308
Fax: (32) 2 538 0841
E-mail: jean.de.lannoy@euronet.be
http://www.jean-de-lannoy.be

CANADA
Renouf Publishing Company Limited
5369 Chemin Canotek Road
CDN-OTTAWA, Ontario, K1J 9J3
Tel.: (1) 613 745 2665
Fax: (1) 613 745 7660
E-mail: order.dept@renoufbooks.com
http://www.renoufbooks.com

CZECH REPUBLIC/
RÉPUBLIQUE TCHÈQUE
USIS, Publication Service
Havelkova 22
CZ-130 00 PRAHA 3
Tel./Fax: (420) 2 2423 1114

DENMARK/DANEMARK
Munksgaard
35 Norre Sogade, PO Box 173
DK-1005 KØBENHAVN K
Tel.: (45) 7 733 3333
Fax: (45) 7 733 3377
E-mail: direct@munksgaarddirect.dk
http://www.munksgaarddirect.dk

FINLAND/FINLANDE
Akateeminen Kirjakauppa
Keskuskatu 1, PO Box 218
FIN-00381 HELSINKI
Tel.: (358) 9 121 41
Fax: (358) 9 121 4450
E-mail: akatilaus@stockmann.fi
http://www.akatilaus.akateeminen.com

FRANCE
C.I.D.
131 boulevard Saint-Michel
F-75005 PARIS
Tel.: (33) 01 43 54 47 15
Fax: (33) 01 43 54 80 73
E-mail: cid@msh-paris.fr

GERMANY/ALLEMAGNE
UNO Verlag
Proppelsdorfer Allee 55
D-53115 BONN
Tel.: (49) 2 28 94 90 231
Fax: (49) 2 28 21 74 92
E-mail: unoverlag@aol.com
http://www.uno-verlag.de

GREECE/GRÈCE
Librairie Kauffmann
Mavrokordatou 9
GR-ATHINAI 106 78
Tel.: (30) 1 38 29 283
Fax: (30) 1 38 33 967

HUNGARY/HONGRIE
Euro Info Service
Hungexpo Europa Kozpont ter 1
H-1101 BUDAPEST
Tel.: (361) 264 8270
Fax: (361) 264 8271
E-mail: euroinfo@euroinfo.hu
http://www.euroinfo.hu

ITALY/ITALIE
Libreria Commissionaria Sansoni
Via Duca di Calabria 1/1, CP 552
I-50125 FIRENZE
Tel.: (39) 556 4831
Fax: (39) 556 41257
E-mail: licosa@licosa.com
http://www.licosa.com

NETHERLANDS/PAYS-BAS
De Lindeboom Internationale
Publikaties
PO Box 202, MA de Ruyterstraat 20 A
NL-7480 AE HAAKSBERGEN
Tel.: (31) 53 574 0004
Fax: (31) 53 572 9296
E-mail: lindeboo@worldonline.nl
http://home-1-worldonline.nl/~linde-boo/

NORWAY/NORVÈGE
Akademika, A/S Universitetsbokhandel
PO Box 84, Blindern
N-0314 OSLO
Tel.: (47) 22 85 30 30
Fax: (47) 23 12 24 20

POLAND/POLOGNE
Głowna Księgarnia Naukowa
im. B. Prusa
Krakowskie Przedmiescie 7
PL-00-068 WARSZAWA
Tel.: (48) 29 22 66
Fax: (48) 22 26 64 49
E-mail: inter@internews.com.pl
http://www.internews.com.pl

PORTUGAL
Livraria Portugal
Rua do Carmo, 70
P-1200 LISBOA
Tel.: (351) 13 47 49 82
Fax: (351) 13 47 02 64
E-mail: liv.portugal@mail.telepac.pt

SPAIN/ESPAGNE
Mundi-Prensa Libros SA
Castelló 37
E-28001 MADRID
Tel.: (34) 914 36 37 00
Fax: (34) 915 75 39 98
E-mail: libreria@mundiprensa.es
http://www.mundiprensa.com

SWITZERLAND/SUISSE
BERSY
Route d'Uvrier 15
CH-1958 LIVRIER/SION
Tel.: (41) 27 203 73 30
Fax: (41) 27 203 73 32
E-mail: bersy@freesurf.ch

UNITED KINGDOM/ROYAUME-UNI
TSO (formerly HMSO)
51 Nine Elms Lane
GB-LONDON SW8 5DR
Tel.: (44) 171 873 8372
Fax: (44) 171 873 8200
E-mail: customer.services@theso.co.uk
http://www.the-stationery-office.co.uk
http://www.itsofficial.net

UNITED STATES and CANADA/
ÉTATS-UNIS et CANADA
Manhattan Publishing Company
468 Albany Post Road, PO Box 850
CROTON-ON-HUDSON,
NY 10520, USA
Tel.: (1) 914 271 5194
Fax: (1) 914 271 5856
E-mail: Info@manhattanpublishing.com
http://www.manhattanpublishing.com

STRASBOURG
Librairie Kléber
Palais de l'Europe
F-67075 STRASBOURG Cedex
Fax: (33) 03 88 52 91 21

Council of Europe Publishing/Editions du Conseil de l'Europe
F-67075 Strasbourg Cedex
Tel.: (33) 03 88 41 25 81 – Fax: (33) 03 88 41 39 10
E-mail: publishing@coe.int – Web site: http://book.coe.fr